C0-AWX-459

We Christians and Jews

The Catholic
Theological Union
LIBRARY
Chicago, Ill.

We CHRISTIANS and JEWS

PAUL J. KIRSCH

The Catholic
Theological Union
LIBRARY
Chicago, Ill.

FORTRESS PRESS

Philadelphia

COPYRIGHT © 1975 BY FORTRESS PRESS

All rights reserved. No part of this publication may be reproduced, stored in a retrieval system, or transmitted in any form or by any means, electronic, mechanical, photocopying, recording, or otherwise, without the prior permission of the copyright owner.

Library of Congress Catalog Card Number 74–26332

ISBN 0–8006–1094–6

4691L74   Printed in the United States of America   1–1094

*For Florrie and Joe
who gave us
Audrey*

CONTENTS

PREFACE

The Catholic
Theological Union
LIBRARY
Chicago, Ill.

As far as I can recall, it was in late 1966 that I first began to think that I wanted to make a contribution to improving understanding between Christians and Jews. The Board of College Education of the Lutheran Church in America and the Faculty Research Fund of Wagner College made possible a visit to Israel in the summer of 1967, under the auspices of the America-Israel Cultural Foundation. Under the same auspices, I made visits also to Geneva and Rome, where I began to study Jewish, Protestant, and Catholic approaches to better understanding.

In the meantime, I had begun to receive the encouragement and assistance of Rabbi Solomon S. Bernards, Director of the Department of Interreligious Cooperation of the Anti-Defamation League of B'nai B'rith, who has become a dear friend. Through Rabbi Bernards's good offices, I participated in a seminar at Vanderbilt Divinity School in Nashville in 1970 and in two seminars at Princeton Theological Seminary in Princeton in 1973 and 1974, seminars co-sponsored by the Anti-Defamation League in which college instructors and ministers come together annually to study Judaism and ways of maturing their presentations of it. Both the study and the conversations with rabbis and other scholars have been invaluable. I have received similar benefit from participation in a dialogue sponsored by the American Jewish Committee and the Lutheran Council in the U.S.A. in Columbus, Ohio, in 1973.

Since 1970, I have taught a course on Judaism at Wagner College, and my students have convinced me many times over that Christians (and some Jews too!) are not only uninformed about Judaism, but also very much delighted to be led into appreciation of it.

Rabbi Bernards has kindly read this essay in manuscript in response to my concern that it be reasonably correct wherever it presumes to describe Jewish perceptions. I want to state my gratitude to him in the strongest terms without at all implicating him in any interpretations that I have made, which are entirely my responsibility.

The Senior Editor of Fortress Press, the Rev. Norman A. Hjelm, has been most gracious in his encouragement of this project and in his helpful suggestions.

Finally, I want to thank my wife, Audrey, for her indispensable work at the typewriter in helping me to get this essay ready, and both Audrey and our daughter Linda for their heart-warming enthusiasm for the idea of it.

INTRODUCTION

"The Jews can never be forgiven for what they did to Jesus until they accept Him as the True Savior." This formulation of a specific kind of Christian opinion was used by Charles Y. Glock and Rodney Stark as a test item in preparing their study of antisemitism.* More than half the Protestants sampled in their survey indicated that they held this proposition to be at least possibly true, and many of those questioned were sure it was true.

There is, of course, a fundamental defect in the form of the proposition, in that it lumps all Jews of the past and present together into one "person." How can persons alive today be either forgiven or *not* forgiven for something done to Jesus long ago by other persons? This objection would no doubt be sustained by any rational person who would give it a moment's thought. Therefore the people who say the proposition is true must be affirming something else. What they mean to say is that Jews of *today* can never be forgiven for what they themselves have done with reference to Jesus "until they accept Him as the

*Charles Y. Glock and Rodney Stark, *Christian Beliefs and Anti-Semitism* (New York: Harper & Row, 1966), p. 61.

1

True Savior." And what they themselves have done to Jesus that calls for forgiveness is, up to this point, *not* to have accepted him as the "True Savior." In other words, there is only one way to be saved and that is by Jesus, and Jews who are not saved by faith in Jesus are not saved. This is the belief of particularist Christianity. "Particularists" are persons who believe that there is only one belief-system according to which persons can be saved, namely, their own.

Thus there are Christians who totally reject the validity of Jewish faith and whose attitudes toward Jews flow from or are consistent with this rejection. On the other hand, we live in an ecumenical age, a time marked by more friendliness and less competitiveness among religious communities. People go about with the tusks and spines of their religious particularity less sharp, less at the ready, and most of us seem to be pleased about that.

One can read this fact negatively, as a function of a general decline of religious conviction and religious seriousness. But to take that line is not to do justice to the tremendous investment that religious groups have made in ecumenism as itself an expression of religious conviction, as an act of obedience to the will of God.

Strictly speaking, "ecumenism" is a word that Christians invented for a project intended to bring about *Christian* unity. The project was a response to a rising consciousness of scandal that, in the face of Jesus' prayer "that they may all be one" (John 17:21), Christians were still divided into so many denominations. There is a sense, then, in which ecumenism is, by definition, a Christian concern, and non-Christians are naturally not expected to have a part in it.

But it comes as no surprise that the complex causes of Christian ecumenism include factors able to produce a wider kind of ecumenism. Since the term "ecumenism" comes from a Greek word referring to the whole inhabited world, it can function just as well in the wider sense. As such, it contemplates questions like these: Can *all* the various religions of the inhabited world "get together"? Are the different religions really different roads up the same mountain—the knowledge and service of the one God—and thus destined to draw closer together the higher they get? Are all religions "true" in their way?

At least by the time that such questions come within sight, and probably much sooner, some Christians will ask about the Jews. "After all," they will say, "where did we get the Ten Commandments and the prophets and the Psalms? We Christians obviously have a connection with Judaism. But how should we define it? What kind of an 'understanding' do we have with the Jews?"

Particularism and ecumenism—these two attitudes in various proportions characterize all Christian communities. That they do so constitutes the dilemma, not to say confusion, in which many Christians find themselves with reference to Jews. They are without clear guidance from the leadership and the theology of their communities. They are subject to the unchallenged influence of particularist elements in their communities, some of which verge on being antisemitic. Their ecumenical feelings toward Jews and the questions that their feelings suggest are given little encouragement. It is true that many church bodies have declared themselves opposed to antisemitism. But that hardly meets the need. Even if such pronouncements significantly reduce the incidence of antisemitism, they fall short of affirming the legitimacy and validity before God of Jewish religion, and thus they fail to challenge antisemitism at its deepest level.

Can it be expected that the spirit of ecumenism abroad in the churches will of itself produce Christian understanding and acceptance of Jewish religiousness? Has it been able to do so? To a degree, no doubt. The spirit of ecumenism has produced a conspicuous increase in the amount and quality of fraternization among Christian and Jewish congregations and clergy. A Jewish congregation will invite a neighboring Christian congregation to share in a *Seder*, and thus the two congregations relive as Christians and Jews together the great model event of God's mercy, the exodus from Egypt. Rabbis will be invited to join the local association of clergy and have monthly fellowship with their Protestant and Catholic counterparts. Rabbis and priests and ministers will organize neighborhood services of worship for Thanksgiving Day and will share in the officiating.

These kinds of events are a "grass roots" response to the spirit of ecumenism; that is, they are local and spontaneous. By the same token, they are not occurring in all cities and towns. They are also unofficial; that is, they have not been institutionalized or even encouraged by the denominations. The reason they have not is that the national governing bodies of the denominations, Christian and Jewish, have no policy and no rationale for such events. What is lacking is a cooperatively worked out theoretical or even theological understanding of who we Christians and Jews are to each other. This book is itself a kind of open letter, pleading that at long last we Christians and Jews come to an understanding of who we are to one another. Much is involved in such a venture, and much is at stake.

1

ESTRANGEMENT

Christianity and Judaism have a considerable overlap, as we have already noted. Their common identification with Abraham, Moses, the prophets, and the psalms would seem to suggest that if any two religions anywhere can come to an understanding about what they have in common and about what they can do together, it ought to be Christianity and Judaism—so we trust it will be. But one has to face the fact that no two religions have had a longer or more intense history of estrangement and mutual recrimination than these two. Christianity and Judaism have lived side by side and in each other's presence for nineteen hundred years and throughout that span have continually contested as to which was the true heir of the covenant with the Father. If we ever hope, in an ecumenical spirit, to overcome this estrangement, we must begin by understanding it.

Estrangement began in the period immediately following the resurrection as the natural falling out of two religious communities, each of which saw itself as the people of God, *the people*, of the one and only God.

The Apostle Paul is a good example of the tensions of the time. The earliest moment of his life that is reported to us is as a student in Jerusalem and presumably a candidate for the rabbinate, for he was studying with Gamaliel, a foremost rabbinical teacher. Saul (Paul) tells us in his letter to the Galatians that he was a Pharisee, and that means that he was scrupulous to obey the Mosaic law, written and oral, as the clear statement of the will of God. In his zeal for Judaism, he actively persecuted the followers of "the way." Why? Although they were Jews and ought to have "known better," they believed that Jesus of Nazareth, who had been crucified, was the Messiah. This must have seemed to Saul at the time to be the height of absurdity. The Messiah was expected to be a king, politically effective by the power of God invested in him, and thus able to bring the kingdoms of this world into conformity with God's will. If the Messiah had in fact come, all peoples ought to have been brought under the reign of peace, justice, and plenty. But actually, not only had no such reign visibly begun, but the Jesus who was being proclaimed as the Messiah had actually been a teacher, not a king, and, what was wider of the mark set by the expectations, had been crucified by the Roman authorities.

So Saul, as a zealous student and a champion of good sense and orthodoxy, had requested letters from the high priest in Jerusalem which authorized him to search out congregations of Christ-worshiping Jews and to bring some of their members to Jerusalem for interrogation, harassment, and possibly penalties (Acts 9:1–2).

The same Saul is pictured in the book of the Acts of the Apostles as having stood by, consenting to what was done, when a Christian deacon named Stephen was stoned to death (Acts 7:58–8:1). Stoning was specified in biblical law as the mandatory punishment for blasphemy (Lev. 24:10–16). Blasphemy is deliberate and outrageous insult to the name of God himself. How had Stephen blasphemed? His message is reported in the book of Acts (Acts 7:1–53). In his own mind, no doubt, it was a forthright proclamation of the gospel, the good news of what

God had done through Jesus, the Son of Man, to bring salvation to all who believed in him. But the speech also included bitter denunciation, not only of those involved in putting Jesus to death, but also of all who failed to see Jesus as the One whom God had promised. It drew the conclusion that the whole history of God's redemptive work among the Jews had been fruitless except for Christianity, that any Jew's failure to see Jesus as the Righteous One proved that that Jew was beyond saving, and that God had in effect withdrawn his concern and grace from all Jews but the followers of Jesus.

Christians have been brought up to know Stephen as "the first Christian martyr" and thus to identify with him emotionally. Even so, it is not impossible for a Christian to put himself in the place of Stephen's Jewish hearers and to feel the bite of what to them was blasphemy, namely, the proposition that God had totally abandoned them. It was not only a flat rejection of their Jewish legitimacy—it was an outrageous denial of the mercy of God toward his elect. Evidently to Saul, too, at the time, it sounded like blasphemy.

Jews who had accepted Jesus as the Christ seemed to Jews who had not to have wandered far afield from Judaism in identifying a crucified teacher as the Messiah. But that could have been tolerated by Judaism because Judaism did not maintain a requirement of strict doctrinal orthodoxy and did not eject anyone from the synagogue for such a vagary of belief. What the Jewish Christians were claiming could even be minimized by Jews as amounting simply to the proposition that the Christians knew who the Messiah was going to be when he came in kingly power, namely Jesus, who had come the first time incognito except among themselves. What was intolerable to Jews was the assertion that God had abandoned his chosen people and replaced them with the followers of Jesus.

On the other hand, from the standpoint of Jews like Stephen, who had become Christians, it was so clear that Jesus as the

Righteous One was God's long-intended completion of the faith of his chosen people that any Jews who did not accept Jesus had displayed invincible spiritual blindness and had disqualified themselves and removed themselves from the number of the chosen people.

Both Jews and Christians, since they believed that there could only be one chosen people, when they claimed the chosen status for themselves, denied it to each other.

It was while Saul was on the road to Damascus with the intention of harassing Christian Jews that he was converted. The book of Acts tells us how he fell to the ground and was blinded and about the voice that addressed him: "Saul, Saul, why do you persecute me?" When Saul asked who was speaking, the voice said, "I am Jesus, whom you are persecuting" (Acts 9:3–5). The upshot was that Saul became a Christian, and beyond that an apostle or missionary for Jesus to the gentiles. Saul evidently had learned a good deal about Jesus in the process of investigating and persecuting those who believed in him. But what was decisive in bringing about his conversion was that Saul had now also become an "eyewitness" to the reality of the resurrection of Jesus, and that the resurrected Jesus himself had called him into his service.

Latecomer though he was to the ranks of the Christian apostles, Saul (now known as Paul) became the most creative and influential theologian among them, and both his thought and his apostolic work had profound consequences for the interrelations of Christians and Jews.

The distinctive character of Paul's apostleship, as he defined it, was that it was addressed to gentiles. This did not mean that Paul as a missionary for Jesus passed by Jews and synagogues. It was his custom, on arriving in a city for the first time, to begin by going to the synagogue and preaching there. But he characteristically lost no time in making contact with the gentiles in marketplaces, public forums, lecture halls, and wherever else he could get an audience. Paul's missionary field was not Palestine —it was Asia Minor, Cyprus, Greece, Macedonia. The cities that he visited, such as Ephesus, Athens, Corinth, Thessalonika, etc., were inhabited predominantly by gentiles, although probably every one of them contained a Jewish colony.

Paul's seeking out of gentiles for conversion was not strange for a teacher brought up as a Jew. Conversion was a major Jewish enterprise at the time. "You traverse sea and land to make a single proselyte," Jesus remarked to some Pharisees (Matt. 23:15). (It was only centuries later that Jews permanently gave up seeking conversions to Judaism because they were expressly compelled to by Christian-sponsored legislation of the Roman empire.)

In seeking conversions Jews were obedient to the universalist thrust of the scriptures. Why had God chosen a people? God said to Abraham, "And I will make of you a great nation . . . and by you all the families of the earth will bless themselves" (Gen. 12:2–3). God said through Moses, ". . . you shall be to me a kingdom of priests . . ." (Exod. 19:6). "It is too light a thing that you should be my servant to raise up the tribes of Jacob and to restore the preserved of Israel; I will give you as a light to the nations, that my salvation may reach to the ends of the earth" (Isa. 49:6). God commanded Jonah, in the didactic story about the prophet Jonah, to preach repentance and salvation to the enemy gentile people of Nineveh in Assyria. And when Jonah sulked because the people listened and repented and were saved, God chided him and said, "And should not I pity Nineveh, that great city, in which there are more than a hundred and twenty thousand persons who do not know their right hand from their left, and also much cattle?" (Jon. 4:11). The point was that all the gods of the gentiles were helpless idols; only the God of Israel was God, and therefore God said, "Turn to me and be saved, all the ends of the earth!" (Isa. 45:22). God would finally be one, according to a rather daring biblical formulation, when all the people of the earth knew he was one and worshiped him alone (Zech. 14:9). Paul justified the out-reach to the gentiles on the basis of similar universalist texts in the Hebrew Bible. (See Rom. 15:8–12.)

What made Paul different from other Jews as a proselytizer of gentiles was that he admitted gentiles into the fellowship of Jesus, into the "Body of Christ," without circumcision and without requiring obedience to the law of Moses. In this Paul was breaking, not only with Jewish practice, but even with previous Christian practice.

We catch a glimpse in the book of Acts of a kind of Christianity that is bound to be unfamiliar to most Christians today. It was the Christianity practiced in Jerusalem under the leadership of the Apostle James, who is identified as "the Lord's brother" (Gal. 1:19). James's style of Christianity was founded on being Jewish in every way and then adding to what being Jewish required: believing that Jesus of Nazareth was the Messiah who had come and was to come again and living by Jesus' midrash on the law of Moses. For example, "You have heard that it was said to the men of old, 'You shall not kill; . . .' But I say to you that everyone who is angry with his brother shall be liable to judgment . . ." (Matt. 5:21–22). James evidently kept on good terms with the Jewish community of Jerusalem as a whole. He represented a kind of Christianity that was a sectarian expression of Judaism and not a departure from Judaism. If we have the picture right, to be a Christian of this sort, a person had to be a Jew first. That is, if anyone proposed to enter *this* Christian community from paganism, he would have had to undergo circumcision and to take upon him the entire yoke of the law of Moses, for example, the Sabbath laws and the dietary laws. But presumably this question did not arise. These Jerusalem Christians would most likely have been the community that preserved the saying attributed to Jesus, "Go nowhere among the Gentiles, and enter no town of the Samaritans . . ." (Matt.

10:5). And when, at a Jerusalem meeting, Paul faced the problem of getting the Apostle James and others like him to accept Paul's missionary work as legitimate, the solution seems to have been that Paul's was a legitimate Christianity for gentiles, though not necessarily for people who had been brought up as Jews (Acts 15:1–35).

If Paul had trouble convincing some Christians that his gentile converts were genuine Christians, it is clear how much more difficult it would have been to convince Jews that his converts were genuine Jews, that is, part of the people of God.

Jews were adamant in requiring circumcision of all who would be the people of Abraham, to whom God had given circumcision as the sign of the covenant. The synagogues in which Paul preached in so many cities of the empire usually were attended by "God-fearers." These were gentiles who were attracted to Jewish monotheism and to Jewish morality and regularly listened to the scriptures and to the instruction in the synagogues. They were the chief reservoir out of which converts to Judaism were drawn, but there is no record and it is really unthinkable that any males were then admitted to Jewry without circumcision. What was true for circumcision was hardly less true for the whole yoke of the law.

The era of Paul was the time of the ascendancy of the Pharisees with their emphasis on obedience to the law as the essence of Judaism. That meant the written law of the scriptures and the oral law which, though still in process at the time of being formulated by the Tannaitic rabbis, was being asserted as stemming equally with the written law from the authority of Moses at Mount Sinai. Yet, here was Paul, the former Pharisee, proclaiming that "Christ is the end of the law, that every one who has faith may be justified" (Rom. 10:4). Paul himself, as a Jew, had access to the preacher's seat in synagogues and was admitted to the temple in Jerusalem for worship. But when it was rumored that he had brought into the temple courtyard, which was reserved for Jews, converts of his from paganism to Christianity, the greatest possible offense was taken by other Jews in the area (Acts 21:27–29). Clearly, as far as Jews were concerned, pagan converts to Paul's teachings did not become Jews and could not be equivalent to Jews in the sight of God.

How did Paul develop his position that gentiles did not need to be Jews first in order to be Christians, but could step directly from paganism into Christianity? Paul explains his reasoning in his Epistle to the Romans. Not only the Jews but all peoples have been endowed by God with a version of God's law. The Jews have the law set forth in the Torah, the gentiles have the law inscribed in their consciences. But neither Jew nor gentile can obey this law of God. "For I do not do the good I want, but the evil I do not want is what I do" (Rom. 7:19). What Paul said about himself he believed to be true of all men. Instead of accomplishing God's project of bringing sinful humanity to the attainment of righteousness, the law had only succeeded in showing to men and women how sin-ridden they were. The law took the measure of sin in the sense of showing its extent; the law did not take the measure of sin in the sense of defeating it.

But, to continue Paul's argument in Romans, God has provided an effective cure for sin. It is a person's faith in Jesus as the Christ, or faith in God at work in Christ. Faith perceives the death of Christ as the perfect sacrifice and expiation for sin and appropriates the benefit of that sacrifice. Thus all a person's guilt and all his deserving of God's retribution are wiped away. But faith does more—it perceives Christ as the perfect embodiment of righteousness and falls in love with that righteousness and identifies all its aspirations with that righteousness, that is, with Christ. Thus there is effected a kind of mystical union of the faithful person and Christ. Christ becomes the dynamic in the depth of the person's being, with the result that he is enabled to be righteous and to do the works of righteousness. "I have been crucified with Christ; it is no longer I who live, but Christ who lives in me . . ." (Gal. 2:20).

Paul's radicalism in rejecting the law makes him a mystery to the Jew. To a devout Jew, the law of God is not a burden, it is a delight; it is not an imposition, but a gift of love. Every aspect of the law has to do with bringing human nature to perfection, in respect to reverence for God, love for neighbor, humaneness, sensitivity, responsiveness, and every positive human potential. What could be more edifying for really human life than to immerse oneself in and to saturate oneself with the law? How then could a Jew like Paul simply throw the law away? The answer seems to be that Paul does not really throw the law away because to Paul Jesus Christ *is* the law in a new and effective form. Paul had thrown away the written and oral law, not as one who no longer believed in its holy purpose, but as one who had found it ineffective to accomplish its purpose. Jews understood the purpose of the law to be to bring the people of God to obedience to God, that is, to righteousness. As a Christian, Paul continued to believe in righteousness as God's purpose for human beings. To transfer his loyalty from the law to Christ was, in his view, to shift from an ineffective means of bringing people to righteousness to an effective one, to one that not only indicated what God's will was, but enabled persons to obey it.

The point can be put more exactly. Rather than to speak of Jewish love and devotion toward the "law," one should speak of Jewish love and devotion toward the Torah. Torah means more than law. It means "instruction from God," and as such has the force of the expressions "revelation" and "Word of God." Jews use it to refer to the Pentateuch, the first five books of the Hebrew Bible. Now Christians and Jews know that the books from Genesis through Deuteronomy contain much more than legislation; they contain narratives that we view as "sacred history," stories about heroes of faith like Abraham and Moses in which God is discerned as playing the decisive role. The story of the exodus from Egypt is one of these. The value of the story is that it proclaims God's grace and mercy as the one who conceived, planned, and engineered the escape from Egypt, working through Moses, his chosen instrument. All the stories that constitute "sacred history" are similar in that they all proclaim the mercy of God. Thus it can be said that Torah embraces both law and "gospel."

The gospel, the "good news," is the sacred story of God's work in history, showing mercy, saving his people. The law, that is, the legislation, the Ten Commandments and the rest, is the guidance as to how the redeemed may show their gratitude and meet God's expectations that they fulfill themselves in attaining righteousness.

Thus it is meaningful to say that for Paul Jesus Christ was the Torah fulfilled; the ultimate Torah was Jesus Christ. The whole Jewish love for the Torah could flow for Paul as love for Christ. Jesus was the new sacred history, God's action in history, in death and resurrection, to wipe out our transgressions, to liberate us from the power of sin, and to bring us to righteousness. Jesus was likewise the new legislation, the human embodiment of God's law. Like the old law, he proved to us that we were sinners and brought us to repentance and forgiveness. Unlike the old law (and here Paul broke with the Pharisees), Jesus became a dynamic within us, through our faith in him, and actually and progressively enabled us to achieve righteousness.

A modern Jew, if he is told that a Christian feels about Christ the way he—the Jew—feels about the Torah, can understand how a Christian feels. A modern Christian, if he is told that a Jew feels about the Torah the way he—the Christian—feels about Christ, can understand how a Jew feels. But it is quite clear that neither Jews nor Christians in Paul's time saw any equivalency here.

1. To the Jew, the gentile Christian was a strange sort of pagan who claimed that he loved the true God, but boldly

rejected the one thing God asked of him, that is, obedience to God's law.

2. To the Jew, the Jewish Christian was at least erratic in mistaking a rabbinical teacher for the Messiah.

3. To the Jew, both gentile and Jewish Christians were absolutely preposterous in claiming that their sect was the true Israel, the new chosen people, and that the historic Jews were not God's people anymore.

4. To the Christian, whether gentile or Jewish, the non-Christian Jew was a strange sort of loser who, after looking for the Messiah for so long, failed to recognize him when he came and forced him to find a new people for his kingdom.

We are left with two religious communities that were actually very close to one another, that for a time actually shared one scripture, the Hebrew Bible, but that were driven apart by incompatible exclusivist claims. Each community saw itself as the true people of the biblical God, and saw its rival as the impostor.

On the Christian side, it was Paul and his school who had certainly aggravated the estrangement by abandoning the Mosaic law as a feature of Christianity and who agonized most about the estrangement and proposed a solution.

There is a very clear assertion in the Epistle to the Romans that the two religious communities, if not essentially one, are aspects of a larger whole that includes them both: all Israel. Paul resorts to analogy: there is a fine old olive tree that has produced great harvests for its owner. But he is aware that there are many wild olive branches in the world that are producing little if anything of worth. So the owner cuts some of these wild olive branches and grafts them onto his productive old tree, where in time they too will produce fine harvests. The old olive tree is the historic chosen people, the Jews. The wild olive branches are gentiles. By means of the ministry of Christ and that of Paul and his sort of apostle, God has detached many gentiles from the sterile trunk of paganism and has grafted them onto the fertile trunk of Judaism. In doing this, God has taken his attention away from his own people for a time, in order to concentrate on gentiles. But that is not to be misunderstood as God's abandonment of his people. After all, he has grafted the pagans onto his historic people. When the grafting has been fully accomplished, God will think again about his people (as modified by the grafting on of gentiles) and in the end, "all Israel will be saved" (Romans 11).

It is true, Paul thinks, that some of the "natural branches" of Israel were broken off "because of their unbelief," but how easily God can graft them back onto the olive tree, if he could graft on *wild* olive branches! (Rom. 11:17–24).

Paul also sees it as providential that many Jews did "trespass," that is, failed to have faith in Jesus, for precisely this has created the opportunity for gentiles to hear the gospel and come to faith in Jesus. Paul even hopes that the success of the gospel among gentiles will "make Israel jealous" and that this will bring Jews to pay more attention to the gospel and then believe in Jesus (Rom. 11:11–12).

In the Epistle to the Ephesians, Paul (or if Paul did not write Ephesians, then Paul's school) takes essentially the same position. Christ has broken down "the middle wall of partition" or "the dividing wall of hostility" between Jews and gentiles, "by abolishing in his flesh the law of commandments and ordinances, that he might create in himself one new man in place of the two, so making peace . . ." (Eph. 2:14–15). In Christ a meeting place has been found where Jews and gentiles can stand together as one and indistinguishable before God. Paul is assuming, of course, that all Jews can join him in embracing Christ as the new and better version of the Torah. He has already seen numerous gentiles embrace the Torah (Jewish monotheism, sacred history, the righteousness of God) in Christ. We will return to Paul's vision later, in order to ask what use of it can be made today. In the decades that followed Paul's ministry, however, it was totally ineffective.

Jews generally could not see Christ as a new and better version of the Torah. They could not see Paul's kind of Christians —those who abandoned the Mosaic *mitzvoth* (commandments), written and oral—as people of God equivalent to themselves. Christians generally, like Paul, could not see Jews as anything but "trespassers" and "unbelievers" for failing to recognize the Messiahship of Jesus. The estrangement of Jews and Christians was established and it has continued in some quarters at least until the present moment.

The separation of Jews and Christians widened as time went by, and their rejection of each other hardened. Paul, who had once persecuted Jews who became disciples of Jesus, fell victim to the same sort of persecution. According to the book of Acts, after Paul had preached in the synagogue in Thessalonika Jews made trouble for him with the local authorities, having him accused of flouting the emperor's laws and asserting that there is a rival king, Jesus (Acts 17:5–9). There are references to other such attacks on Paul (Acts 18:12f, Acts 20:3, Acts 23:12f). Paul's own attitude was not always conciliatory. To the Christian congregation at Philippi he could write, "Look out for the dogs, look out for the evil-workers, look out for those who mutilate the flesh. For we are the true circumcision . . ." (Phil. 3:2–3). That was to say that Jews were evil-workers and that Christians were the *true* Israel.

Other New Testament writers display similar ideas. The author of the Epistle to the Hebrews expressly stated that the new covenant had made the old covenant obsolete (Heb. 8:13). The Gospel of Matthew polemically pictures the Jews of Jerusalem as unitedly and unhesitatingly taking full responsibility for the crucifixion (Matt. 27:25); and by the time the fourth Gospel was written, the fact that Jesus was a Jew almost seems to have been forgotten in the steady identification of the opposition to Jesus simply as "the Jews." In the same mood, many early Christians believed that the fall of Jerusalem in A.D. 70, in a struggle against the Roman empire for independence, was a sign of God's rejection of the Jews for not accepting Jesus as the Messiah (cf. Matt. 21:43).

In a really pluralistic society, that is, a society that tolerates a variety of professions of religion, a society in which the government makes no commitment to sponsor or even to favor one religion and regards all religions with equal favor, competing religions may make mutually contradictory claims to their hearts' content without inducing either bloodshed or loss of civil rights. The competition operates largely in the arena of verbal argument. The early Roman empire approximated such a pluralism, although it did require of all its subjects, in addition to their voluntary religions, participation in the worship of the emperor. For polytheistic citizens it was no great hardship to add one more divinity to the liturgical calendar. And the empire was believed thus to enjoy the favor of all the gods and in addition to profit politically from having one cult in which all citizens were united.

Jews benefited from this pluralistic tolerance during most of the first three centuries of our era, especially in the diaspora. Christians did not. But the time was to come when Christianity would secure the undoing of the pluralism, such as it was, and would become the established religion of the empire. Then it would be difficult for Jews.

Jews had sufficiently established in Roman consciousness, both by martyrdoms and by readiness for martyrdom, that they were incorrigibly monotheist, and thus their inability to worship the emperor was usually acknowledged and accepted. Jews' troubles with the pagan empire rose out of their demand for independence, especially in Palestine. This demand, involved as it was with a messianism which in turn was part and parcel of

Jewish religion, was really religious. But in Roman eyes it appeared sufficiently of a political nature not to lead to any general suppression of synagogue activity. After the Bar Kochba War (A.D. 132–135), the emperor Hadrian did prohibit the practice of the Jewish religion, but the order was enforced only in Galilee, and it was revoked in a few years except for the provision that Jews were forbidden to make converts to Judaism. This law, too, became a dead letter in practice.

In the early first century, when Christians seemed to the Roman authorities to be a sect within Judaism, they seemed on the whole to have enjoyed Jews' privileges in the empire at large. But as Christianity came to be recognized as a distinct religion and as one not officially tolerated, it came under attack. At first the attacks were local, essentially popular rather than governmental, and premised on suspicions and rumors. Christians were accused of hatred of the human race (perhaps because they remained aloof, on moral and religious grounds, from much in the cities' commercial and social life), of atheism (evidently for rejecting idols and the emperor as divine and for worshiping an invisible God), and of cannibalism and incest (because of the sharing of the Eucharist—"the body and blood"—among "brothers and sisters" in closed, nocturnal meetings). The emperor Nero blamed the burning of much of Rome in A.D. 64 on the Christians, and many of them were publicly tortured to death in and outside Nero's gardens on the basis of this charge. Other local persecutions followed at various times, in Antioch, Smyrna, southern Gaul, Egypt, northern Africa, Bithynia, and Pontus.

When Christianity continued to grow rapidly in the cities, it came to the attention of the imperial government itself. What was to become of the supposedly unifying public worship of the emperor, if not only Jews but the vastly more numerous sect of Christians refused to participate? Early in the second century Christians were not hunted down systematically. Sometimes their leaders were, sometimes congregations were because of some public complaint. Once in custody, Christians were required to clear themselves by renouncing Christ and worshiping the emperor—or to pay with their lives. But as the church still continued to grow, the empire was more and more faced with the choice of eliminating emperor-worship or eliminating Christians. The emperor Decius in the mid-third century and the emperors Diocletian and Galerius, from 301 to 310, systematically attempted the latter. Thousands died, but the policy failed. Then the emperor Constantine brought a whole new policy into effect, the turn toward a Christian empire.

There is no reason to think Constantine was religiously insincere and merely political in his conversion to Christianity during his rise to power. But he was an emperor intensely interested in having the empire enjoy "favor in heaven and cohesion on earth." Christianity was a very visible and always growing minority in the urban centers before Constantine. When Constantine's Edict of Milan in 313 made Christianity fully legal and restored the churches and other properties that had been confiscated by persecuting emperors, Christianity became overwhelmingly the popular faith. Constantine clearly favored Christianity by building churches at imperial expense and by making Sunday a holiday. He also made it a crime to become a Jew by conversion. When he became sole emperor in 324, master in the East as well as in the West, he extended his policy as patron of Christianity throughout the empire. In 325, it was he who called the first ecumenical council of Christian bishops, at Nicaea, in an effort to restore Christian unity upset by the Arian controversy and succeeded in uniting the bishops behind the first universally accepted creed.

What was implicit in Constantine's rule became increasingly explicit among his successors. Theodosius I (A.D. 379–395) declared that there was properly only one religion of the empire, the Christian religion, and forbade heathen worship; and although he intervened ten times against local violence that had damaged synagogues, the fact of the damage indicates the climate that had been produced. Theodosius II, emperor in the East from 408 to 450, defined Judaism as a tolerated religion, but stipulated that it must not be permitted to be offensive to Christianity, banned conversions to Judaism, forbade the construction of new synagogues, ordered the destruction of unsafe synagogues unless disorder would result, forbade Jews to hold high office, either civil or military, or to have any jurisdiction over Christians, and abolished the office of the Patriarch, the universally recognized arbiter of questions of Jewish practice.

This was the beginning of an erosion of Jewish rights that continued apace in Europe, with occasional remissions, until Hitler decided Jews had not even the right to exist.

St. John Chrysostom (A.D. 344–407) is representative among the church fathers of the extremes of anti-Jewish diatribe of which the church was capable and by which the Roman empire and populace were inflamed. Chrysostom gave strong utterance to the charge against the Jews of *deicide* and asserted that for this crime there was no possible atonement or forgiveness: God will hate and punish the Jews until the end of the world, and Christians should deport themselves accordingly. A striking aspect of this anti-Jewish expression is that it mentions no current offensiveness of Jewish behavior. Over and above its finding all Jews guilty of the death of Jesus, what it does is to seize on every item of criticism that Moses and the prophets laid on ancient Israelites and apply these also in exaggerated terms to every contemporary Jew. Totally forgotten was the fact that what was being cited was Hebrew *self-criticism*.

In any other perspective, the biblical people win high marks for producing the prophets, and for the prophets' bold application to community life of the lofty demands of the God of righteousness. In this, the prophets set the standard of ethical religion that Jesus and others represented in their times. Every

Christian tradition that has taken the prophets and Jesus seriously has made the same kind of criticism of the immorality of *its own* society. Furthermore prophetic religion, both Jewish and Christian, has always joined denunciation of evil behavior with a call to repentance and a reminder of God's promise of forgiveness. But Chrysostom's sermons against the Jews select all biblical promises of redemption for the exclusive possession of Christians and all biblical threats and judgments for exclusive application to Jews.

Chrysostom was evidently provoked in part by ongoing Jewish proselytism and its successes. Even the very presence of Jews raised an awkward question: "If the Messiah has indeed come, why don't the Jews know it? He was promised to them. If Jesus was the Messiah, why are there still Jews?" Augustine's (A.D. 354–430) answer was all too convincing for Christians and damaging to Jews: the Jews will be saved at the end of time, as Paul taught; but in the meantime they must *witness* by their sufferings to God's wrath against those who reject his Son. Augustine's conclusion: Christians must love Jews and lead them into Christianity, but in the meantime they must expect to see Jews hounded by the wrath of God. Augustine was remembered better as proclaiming God's wrath against Jews as Jews than as calling for Christian love toward Jews.

The legal status of Jews continued to decline in both Christian East and Christian West. The sixth-century Code of Justinian in the East retracted the status of Judaism as a tolerated religion. In the seventh century, the emperor Heraclius required all Jews to be baptized, and only the invasions of the Muslims saved them. In the West, the barbarian invasions and the kingdoms they carved out of the empire had largely negative effects on Jewish status. Each Jewish community had to bargain for whatever kind of civil rights and protection it could get. In some cases, Jews virtually became the property of Christian rulers, enjoying official protection in exchange for heavy and arbitrary taxation. The Visigothic king of Spain, Sisebut (A.D. 612–621), became the next but not the last ruler to demand of Jews that they choose either to be baptized or to be expelled from the country. Agobard, the ninth-century archbishop of Lyons, found his ruler, the son of Charlemagne, too indulgent toward Jews and too protective of their liberties, and he revived the excoriating anti-Jewish preaching of Chrysostom.

The continued anti-Jewish preaching of churchmen coupled with suspicions about Jewish sympathy with the Muslims, under whose rule Jews had fared better in East and West, led to the monstrous crimes against Jews unleashed by the Crusades. The Crusaders were summoned to liberate the Holy Land and its shrines from the "infidel" Muslims, many of whom had preyed on Christian pilgrims. Once on their way, less disciplined Crusaders were seized by the thought sometimes planted by Christian preachers that they ought to deal first with the "infidels" in their midst. Beginning at Rouen in 1096 and continuing down the Rhine and the Danube valleys, in town after town they fanatically offered Jews the choice of baptism or massacre. Some accepted baptism, some committed suicide, thousands were slaughtered in spite of efforts by many clergy and laity to hide and protect them. The second crusade, in 1146, provided a repetition of these atrocities.

The accusations of ritual murder of Christians made against various Jewish communities beginning in the twelfth century, preposterous as they are, the charge that Jews fiendishly desecrated the host, the allegations that Jews conspired to poison Christians' wells and were responsible for the Black Death in the fourteenth century, all of which caused the massacre of thousands, further contributed to the degradation of the image of the Jew. The Fourth Lateran Council (1215) introduced to Christendom the requirement that Jews wear distinctive dress. The yellow badge in France, the peculiarly shaped hat in Germany and Poland, and other items elsewhere tended to make defenseless Jews all the more the targets of ridicule and abuse. Thus even bishops are seen to have been caught up in the general fear and hatred of Jews. It is sometimes claimed that the exorbitant rates of interest charged by Jewish lenders was the real cause of medieval animosity. But even this situation is rooted in religious resentment. It was for reasons of religion that Jews had been forbidden to own slaves when everyone else might and were thus forced out of agriculture. It was for reasons of religion that Jews had been banned from the legal profession, from public and military offices, and numerous other occupations—any in which they exercised authority over Christians. Jews were drawn into money-lending by the facts that usury (or interest taking) was forbidden to Christians and that someone had to lend money. Time and again the pattern was repeated that Christian rulers set the interest rates, set them high because otherwise so risky a business was not profitable enough to be inviting, taxed the profits heavily, and then periodically expelled all Jews, confiscating their property. About as often, the expulsion was followed in a few years by a recall of the expelled; they were a necessity to the royal economy. It says much about the universal precariousness of Jewish existence in Europe, that the expelled would be found willing to believe promises and to return and begin again in places where they had been robbed and expelled.

In 1290, the Jews of England, having been completely stripped of their property, were expelled from England "permanently." In 1391, Spanish Jews were offered the choice between death and baptism. In 1394, Jews were expelled from France. Germany and Italy, not being unified, could only expel Jews city by city and did so. In 1492, Jews were expelled from Spain. Even the *Marranos* (Jews who had accepted baptism but continued to be Jews privately while Christians publicly) were so threatened as heretics by the Spanish Inquisition that they too fled. Many of those who remained in Europe settled in Poland, where they enjoyed relative security till the massacres of the middle seventeenth century.

The Reformation of the sixteenth century made little difference for Jews. In his early years as a reformer, Martin Luther denounced the typical Christian treatment of Jews and thought it was no wonder that Jews were not won over to Christianity. He expected the church of the Reformation to win the Jews as converts. When it became apparent that it would not, Luther became as violent against the Jews as Chrysostom and reached a larger audience.

We have seen that the separation, the estrangement, from each other of Jews and Christians was essentially religious. There could be only one chosen people, but there were two claimants to the title and each was a blasphemous impostor to the other.

Every dreadful charge against Jews, such as deicide, follows from this religious alienation and, given the fact that Christianity and not Judaism got hold of the power of the state, every dreadful thing that has since happened in Europe to Jews as a people equally follows from this alienation.

No wonder Reinhold Niebuhr was moved to say that Christians have forfeited for all time to come the right to speak to Jews about the God of love.

If no estrangement from Judaism had developed, Christianity might have remained a Jewish sect, small, obscure, without its productive gentile mission. It might have had an effect on Judaism, but only indirectly on the world. With Christianity's estrangement from Judaism, the world inherited the immensely successful gentile mission, the Christian church, and the universal outreach of a monotheism focused on the God who had once been known only as God of the Jews. If only the estrangement which produced two religions of great worth had not produced Christian animosity, the death of pluralism in Europe, and the use of the power of the state to attack Jews, how much less regretfully Christians today could read the history of the West.

2

MESSIAH

The identification of Jesus as the Messiah was a primary factor in the divergence and estrangement from each other of early Christianity and the Judaism of the time. To many, it seems to be the chief distinction between the two communities today. The difference is sharply put in a frequently quoted statement by Martin Buber, an influential Jewish philosopher (1878–1965) who thought much about the interrelationship of Jews and Christians. "Pre-Messianically our destinies are divided," Buber wrote. "Now to the Christian the Jew is the incomprehensibly obdurate man, who declines to see what has happened [namely, that the Messiah has come]; and to the Jew the Christian is the incomprehensibly daring man who affirms in an unredeemed world that its redemption has been accomplished."*

One thing not in dispute is that the idea of the Messiah originates and is developed in the Hebrew Bible, more specifically in the texts of the literary prophets. Let us look at some of the most important of these texts and review the contents of the term.

---

* Lily Edelman (ed.), *Face to Face* ("Jewish Heritage," vol. 9, no. 4 [Washington: B'nai B'rith, 1967]), p. 18.

"Messiah" is an adaptation in spelling and pronunciation of the Hebrew *Mashiach* meaning "anointed one." Since anointing was the Hebrew cultural equivalent of crowning, an anointed one was a king. However, in the restricted sense of God's anointed, or anointed by God, the term was reserved increasingly for an ideal king in the indefinite future who would establish a kind of golden age.

One of the more familiar early references to the Messiah is recorded in Isaiah 9.

> The people who walked in darkness
>   have seen a great light;
> those who dwelt in a land of deep darkness,
>   on them has light shined.
> Thou hast multiplied the nation,
>   thou hast increased its joy;
> they rejoice before thee
>   as with joy at the harvest,
>   as men rejoice when they divide the spoil.
> For the yoke of his burden,
>   and the staff for his shoulder,
>   the rod of his oppressor,
>   thou hast broken as on the day of Midian.
> For every boot of the tramping warrior in battle tumult
>   and every garment rolled in blood
>   will be burned as fuel for the fire.
> For to us a child is born,
>   to us a son is given;
> and the government will be upon his shoulder,
>   and his name will be called
>   "Wonderful Counselor, Mighty God,
>   Everlasting Father, Prince of Peace."
> Of the increase of his government and of peace
>   there will be no end,
> upon the throne of David, and over his kingdom,
>   to establish it, and to uphold it
> with justice and with righteousness
>   from this time forth and for evermore.
> The zeal of the Lord of hosts will do this." (Isa. 9:2–7)

The tense is interesting. It appears that the prophet is pointing to an event that has already happened. Nevertheless, we are assured that he was heard as pointing to an indefinite future.

What kind of future is the prophet thinking of? To a degree it depends on how figurative his language was intended to be. One possibility clearly is that he is thinking of an actual Israelite king, a human being who with the help of God will establish politically the kind of justice and peace God wants people to enjoy in this world. Another possibility is that the poem must be taken more symbolically and less literally. However, given the absence of any evidence of Hebrew belief in an other-worldly heaven in Isaiah's time, the imagery must have reference to a this-worldly ideal.

Some of the same possibilities exist in connection with the poem in Isaiah 11, verses 1–9. The lines given to describing the Messiah himself can be applied to a king or possibly to a spiritual leader. The lines beginning with verse 6, that have the leopard lying down with the kid, seem more emphatically to demand a nonliteral reading. For example, this may be poetic imagery for the notion that predatory traits in human beings will be overcome and that the human world will be safe for the innocent. Again, so far as the prophet's intentions are determinative of the meaning, it cannot be thought that the reference is to an other-worldly heaven.

Psalm 2 is of special interest in this connection. It is sometimes thought of as a coronation hymn, suggesting that it may have been composed and used originally for the ceremony in which actual kings of Israel or Judah were anointed. The words "You are my son, today I have begotten you," then expressed the conviction that God adopted the king, at the moment of his anointing, as his son. This must be construed as saying that the king is God's honorary son. The alternative, the implication of a supernatural origin for the Hebrew king is simply not supported by anything in the biblical literature. Whether this psalm began its career as a coronation hymn and then was reinterpreted as referring to the Messiah, or whether it was always considered to be a hymn about the Messiah, the most the psalm was understood as claiming is that the Messiah is a human king, and is an honorary son of God, and God will give him victory over his enemies, rulers of the earth.

There are numerous other references to the Messiah that for the most part echo the ones we have reviewed. In the oracles of the Second Isaiah, however, we have a unique line of thought. The writer identifies a king of his own time, and not a Hebrew but a Persian king, Cyrus, as the Messiah.

By unanimous consent, the composer of the oracles attributed to the "Second Isaiah" (Isaiah 40–55) is one of the greatest of the prophets. In contrast with most prophets, he was inspired to recognize in his time a moment not of divine judgment but of salvation, that is, the end of the Babylonian captivity. He reveals repeatedly in his choice of imagery that he likens the imminent return from Babylonia to Jerusalem, which was to begin in 538 B.C., to the exodus from Egypt, up till then the supreme paradigm of God's grace. As he prophesies, the prophet is a member of the exiled community resident in Babylonia. He sees the extraordinarily successful and humane empire-builder Cyrus of Persia about to challenge the Babylonians. He foresees not only that Cyrus will inherit the Babylonian empire, but that when he does he will invite the Jewish exiles to return to their home territory in Judah. "Comfort, comfort . . ., he cries. "Speak tenderly to Jerusalem and cry to her . . . that her iniquity is pardoned . . ." (Isa. 40:1–2).

The prophet stands within the great tradition of discerning sacred history or salvation history. The God of Israel is the Lord of history. Cyrus is therefore no accident. He is the appointed agent of the God of Israel to effect the end of the compulsory exile and to make possible the restoration in Jerusalem. Just as Isaiah of Jerusalem almost two centuries earlier had seen the great empire of the Assyrians as "the rod of Yahweh's anger," that is, as God's instrument for the punishment of Israel, so now the Isaiah of the exile sees Cyrus as the staff of Yahweh's blessing. And he calls Cyrus God's anointed, that is, Messiah. The prophet's usage, applying the title "Messiah" to a man of his own time and to a non-Hebrew, indicates the non-standardization of the term and the flexibility with which it could be used, as well as reenforcing the impression that the expected referent for the title was a this-worldly king.

In the next generation, among the Hebrews who had returned to Jerusalem, a similar term, "The Branch" (of the House of David), was used in reference to Zerubbabel. The Hebrews in Jerusalem were still subjects of the Persian empire. But at least some in the prophetic community saw this contemporary member of the royal family as anointed by God to lead his people forward to complete independence.

Curiously, the Maccabean War for independence against the tyranny of Antiochus Epiphanes in the second century B.C. produced no surviving texts that invoked the Messiah. For the war against Antiochus was not only a war for independence but a religious war, for it aimed at freedom from the oppression of an emperor who had determined to stamp out Jewish religion. Antiochus believed that the security of his empire required all his subjects to conform to one religion—of his choice—a Hellenistic version of Greek polytheism in which Antiochus himself was to be revered as a manifestation of Zeus. Some Jews were frightened into accepting Antiochus' demands, for he sent his troops throughout Judah confiscating copies of the Torah and forcing Jewish people by the sword to perform sacrifices to himself. But a desperate armed rebellion, led by Judas Maccabeus and subsequently by others of his family, succeeded beyond what could have been the wildest hopes at the beginning and won the independence of a territory almost equivalent to the ancient kingdom of Solomon.

The rabbis of the subsequent period created the festival of Hanukkah to celebrate this triumph; they centered the observance on the liberation of the temple in Jerusalem and its rededication after it had been purged of all relics of Antiochus, who had had it used for the worship of Zeus. Yet, there is no evidence that any of the Maccabean heroes or kings was hailed as Messiah.

The reason for this may be that Jewish hopes for the future had begun to be expressed in a new key. The beginning of the Maccabean revolt is the time usually assigned for the appearance of the book of Daniel, and Daniel is the classic biblical expression of apocalyptic thinking. For the apocalypticists, the days they were living in were the time of the end of the world as humanity had known it. God had decreed the radical end of the old order and the beginning of the new. Apocalyptic writers deliberately used obscure imagery, probably to keep their message from all but the initiated, and not all of them necessarily had the same vision of what was to come, so that it is difficult to characterize apocalypticism precisely. But for such writers generally, the nature of the changes soon to come is unprecedented. The very ground rules of history are to be different after God has intervened. Tyranny as such will be eliminated and the reign over an innocent and peaceful world will be exercised by "the saints of the Most High" (Dan. 7:27).

This is the connection in which the Messianic title "Son of Man" assumes great importance. The term had been used in the book of Ezekiel the prophet as a title for the prophet himself. In the book of Daniel, the expression "Son of Man" functions as a collective term for the "saints of the Most High," to whom God is to commit the governance of the renewed world; or it functions as the designation of an individual through whom God will bring in the new order of things and who will exercise the dominion of the saints (Dan. 7:13).

The fact that in the Synoptic Gospels Jesus is given the two titles, "Messiah" and "Son of Man," suggests that at least for some in the Jewish community of Jesus' time the two designations had been assimilated to one another. That would mean that all the regal authority of the Messiah effectively to provide a governance of justice and peace in this world could be combined with the unwarlike and even uncoercive character of the "saints of the Most High," who were distinguished by faithful obedience to the charitable will of God. It was possible for the saints, with all their gentleness, to be thought of as ruling the world because God himself was expected under this same rubric to have directly demolished all oppressors and oppression. The notion suggests itself that the drawing together of the concepts "Son of Man" and "Messiah" facilitated the identification of Jesus as Messiah. Certainly there is little in the New Testament recollections of Jesus that casts him, even possibly, in the role of son of David, warrior-king, slayer of the enemies of God, enforcer of order by the power of the sword. There is much in the Gospels, on the other hand, especially in the stories of Jesus feeding the hungry, healing the sick, counseling love, and abstaining from resistance against his enemies, that makes him a paradigm of the "saints of the Most High."

Apocalyptic Jewish thought did not long survive the age of Jesus. The consequence of this was that the more this-worldly and kingly elements in the expectations of the Messiah eclipsed the supernaturalist features of the Son of Man doctrine for mainline Judaism.

The best example of this can be seen in the history of Rabbi Akiba and Simon bar Kochba. The time was about one hundred years after the death and resurrection of Jesus. Although a Jewish war of independence against the Roman empire had failed disastrously in A.D. 70, with measureless loss of life and the destruction of the Second Temple and of Jerusalem itself,

Jewish dreams of independence had not been killed. The Roman imperial oppression in Palestine, more and more reminiscent of Antiochus Epiphanes, attempted to make the very practice of Jewish religion there illegal and provoked another Jewish war for freedom. The leader of the guerrilla-type Jewish forces, Bar Kochba, was as pious as he was courageous and astute. Rabbi Akiba was so impressed by the holiness of the cause and its hope for success that he proclaimed Bar Kochba the Messiah!

Rabbi Akiba (A.D. c.40 to c.135), although not well known to Christians, deserves to be. He was one of the greatest of the rabbis known as Tannaim, immensely authoritative masters of the Torah, teachers of other rabbis, and creators of tradition. The Tannaim, who flourished from the time of Jesus until approximately A.D. 200, are most noteworthy for being the rabbis deemed important enough to be quoted in the Mishnah, the official systematization of the oral law which became the basis and nucleus of the Talmud. Akiba has special distinction among the Tannaim both as one of the inventors of the system according to which the oral law was arranged in the Mishnah and as a martyr. Akiba was tortured to death for defying Roman prohibitions of Jewish religious practices, including even study of the Torah, and probably also because of his relationship with Bar Kochba. He died with the words of the Shema, the Jewish confession of faith, on his lips. Sometime earlier Bar Kochba too had been killed by the Romans, and the military struggle against the Romans was totally defeated.

It is striking that Akiba's identification of Bar Kochba as Messiah, mistaken though it must be judged to have been, did not discredit Akiba himself. His prestige as an innovator and a shaper of Jewish sacred tradition (the oral law) could not be greater than it is. From this we may infer that he was not *badly* mistaken about Bar Kochba as far as classical Judaism, the Judaism that produced the Talmud, was concerned. He evidently had hold of the normative Jewish notion of the Messiah, the "son of David" who sets this world straight by militarily and politically overthrowing tyranny and exploitation.

That Akiba's understanding of what the Messiah was expected to be and to do was typical is supported by the dictum of a rabbi of the following century which was dignified by inclusion in the enormously authoritative Talmud. Said Rabbi Samuel, "There is no difference between this world and the days of the Messiah, except that they will be free of the servitude to the foreign kingdoms."* That is, the days of the Messiah were not imagined as set in another world, in heaven, or "beyond history." They were to unfold in this world, purged of tyranny.

The crushing defeat of Bar Kochba by the Romans and the bitter disappointment of Messianic hopes that was involved had a profound effect on the Jewish consciousness. To think so readily and so eagerly about the days of the Messiah came to be regarded among Tannaitic rabbis as a mistake. Was it not precisely the entertainment of such thoughts that precipitated wars for independence against hopeless odds and wasted the people as well as their substance? So the days of the Messiah tended to be placed in the indefinite future, in God's good time, that is, they would come when God was ready to give them. Thus, not again until the seventeenth century was a living person widely accepted as the Messiah. His name was Shabbetai Tzevi, and it was he who proclaimed that he was the Messiah. It is poignant testimony to the extent of the oppression suffered by Jews all over Europe at the time that Shabbetai Tzevi's proclamation evoked almost incredibly widespread affirmative response. What was looked for from Shabbetai Tzevi fell within the mainstream of expectations of the Messiah. There was to be a peaceful kingdom, centered in Palestine.

Our concern is with the fact that Christians identify Jesus as

*The Judaic Tradition, ed. Nahum N. Glatzer, rev. ed. (Boston: Beacon Press, 1969), p. 239.

the Messiah and Jews do not. How can there be so diametrical a disagreement about a matter of historical fact? So far we have considered the story of how the term "Messiah" was used in the Hebrew Bible and in ancient Judaism. One conclusion that can be drawn is that we are not dealing with a term that has one precise and invariable referent, as though we had to do with the name of a chemical element, like carbon 14. "Messiah" is a symbol for a kind of hope, hope on a grand scale, involving the reordering of all of human life, and in the nature of the case different personalities in different historical settings entertain different versions of what belongs to that hope. It is possible for one person to see an event as fulfilling or promising to fulfill this hope while another does not see it so. Rabbi Akiba saw the Messiah in Bar Kochba; by no means all Jews alive at the time agreed. Simon bar Jonah saw the Messiah in Jesus of Nazareth; by no means all Jews alive at this time agreed. If Rabbi Akiba had lived in Jesus' time and come to know Jesus, he would surely have loved him dearly as a great teacher with a sure grasp of what was central, but it is unimaginable that he would have thought of him as the Messiah.

Most Christians have not been prepared to see this matter in this way. They have heard so many prophecies from the Hebrew Bible in the Christmas and Easter liturgies and heard them interpreted so repeatedly as pointing precisely to Jesus that they are not prepared to imagine how any but the willfully blind could have failed to see that Jesus was the Messiah. They have been so over-assured that the case for the Messiahship of Jesus was unanswerable that they have never really examined the case. But if we were to reopen the question today, many Christians would not only concede that there was room for honest differences of opinion, but might also wonder if *they* would have been found among the believers if they had lived at the time.

Here, for the sake of discussion, is a possible solution of this conflict of opinions in the form of a paradox: Christians are right in asserting that Jesus is the Christ; Jews are right in asserting that Jesus is not the Messiah.

What makes this sound like a self-contradiction is the fact that the term "Christ" is literally equivalent to the term "Messiah." As we saw, *Mashiach* is Hebrew for "anointed one." *Christos* is Greek for "anointed one." Originally then these two terms were absolute equivalents, and Christians have the custom of using "Christ" rather than "Messiah" only because the New Testament was written in Greek, and when it was translated "*Christos*" was rendered as "Christ," not as "Messiah."

But as the decades and then the centuries of Christian history came and went, the term "Christ" underwent some changes of meaning. Instead of having its meaning controlled by the meaning of "Messiah" and thus pointing to whatever Jews meant by "Messiah," "Christ" acquired connotations and nuances of its own, that corresponded to developing Christian thought about the significance of Jesus. "Christ" came to be a distinctively Christian title and to mean whatever Christians meant by it. That is, "Christ" came to function as a symbol for the whole content of Christian beliefs about Jesus, or better, as a Christian symbol for everything that Jesus really is. If "Christ" stands for everything that Jesus really is, then it is a simple tautology to say that Christians are right in believing that Jesus is the Christ.

By the same logic, since the term "Messiah" was originated by the Jews and remains significant to them, it can be said to mean whatever Jews mean by it. Since what Jews mean by "Messiah" is demonstrably something other than what Jesus is, Jews are right in asserting that Jesus is not the Messiah.

We have seen above that the term "Messiah," being the symbol for a hope, has been imprecise and poetic and has conjured up somewhat different ideals in various ages. In modern times, for example, Reform Judaism has felt free to abandon the notion of the Messiah as a person—a king—and has substituted the idea of the Messianic age, a time when dreams of peace with justice will have come true for all mankind under whatever leadership or form of government. But with all the variations, a consistent feature of Jewish Messianic thought remains: when one talks about the days of the Messiah one is talking about this world and the actual achievement of the Golden Age in it. If one concedes to Jews the right to mean what they please by their own term "Messiah," according to the rules of their own discourse, then it follows that one cannot be offended or surprised that in such discourse Jesus is not the Messiah.

One consequence of our discussion thus far may be summarized as follows: whether one can honestly call Jesus the Messiah or the Christ depends entirely on what these titles mean to one; and what these titles mean to persons and communities necessarily varies, because in the nature of things there is no way to establish a single, standardized, "correct" meaning.

There are numerous implications here for the interpretation of the Gospels, but particularly for the understanding of the suffering and death of Jesus. Probably the worst of the allegations that Jews have had to live with in Christian lands for nineteen hundred years are the assertions that "the Jews can never be forgiven for what they did to Jesus until they accept Him as the True Savior," and "the reason the Jews have so much trouble is because God is punishing them for rejecting Jesus." (These are the forms of the propositions that were used in the study, mentioned earlier, *Christian Beliefs and Anti-Semitism*, by Charles Y. Glock and Rodney Stark, pp. 61 and 63, according to which more than half of all American Protestants affirm the first formula and more than one-third affirm the second as at least possibly true.)

Let us review, in reference to these allegations, the kinds of observations that follow from the analysis given above and similar analyses.

1. One cannot truthfully say that "the Jews" rejected or did anything else to Jesus. The expression "the Jews" is too inclu-

sive. In fact almost any sentence the subject of which is "the
Jews" turns out to be false. Most of the Jews alive in the world
at the time of Jesus lived outside Palestine and probably had not
even heard of Jesus when he died. Of the Jews living in Palestine then, those who heard of Jesus flocked to him in great numbers and heard him gladly. It was impossible for the chief
priests to arrest Jesus on one occasion when he was preaching in
the temple area because "they feared the multitudes, because
they held him to be a prophet" (Matt. 21:46). The persons
who became disciples and apostles of Jesus and in time the substance of earliest Christianity were all Jews. It is therefore as
true to say that Jews accepted Jesus as to say that Jews rejected
Jesus.

2. "The Jews can never be forgiven for what they did to
Jesus. . . ." The formula illicitly lumps all Jews, past, present,
and future into one legal "person." To raise the question
whether this entity "can be forgiven" is to talk about present
and future Jews. To point to "what they did to Jesus" is to talk
about a very small number of Jews nineteen hundred years ago.
How can anyone or a whole people be forgiven today for what
someone else did a long time ago? Does not forgiveness apply
only to the actually guilty? One can savor the full absurdity of
the formula by trying out analogies. The Greeks (all Greeks
past, present, and future) can never be forgiven for what they
did to Socrates until they accept him as the only true philosopher. The Americans (all of us) can never be forgiven for what
we did to Abraham Lincoln until we do something or other in
the future.

3. What does it mean to say that Jews "rejected" Jesus?
Probably to most persons it means "did not accept Jesus as the
Messiah." "The Jews can never be forgiven . . . until they accept
Him as the True Savior." But we have looked at this issue and
have already seen that there was and is room for difference of
opinion. The more strictly one adhered to tradition, that is, the

more conservative one was, the more one demanded that anyone being considered as a possible Messiah be a "son of David," that is, militarily and politically as well as morally capable of reforming the world. Such persons would have tended to agree with Rabbi Akiba in recognizing Messianic stature in Simon bar Kochba; by the same token they would have conscientiously resisted anyone's claims that Jesus was the Messiah. Only persons who were willing to rethink the inherited concept of Messiah and to "spiritualize" it were capable of seeing the Messiah in Jesus.

4. "God is punishing [the Jews] for rejecting Jesus." Presumably, according to everything that Christians and Jews believe about morality, God only punishes the wicked. The wicked are those who do evil. Doing evil is human behavior that violates some specifiable moral commandment or rule or value. What is the moral status of not believing what one finds unconvincing, and believing what one cannot help finding persuasive? Some persons may think that the issue here is not a moral one at all. Others may think that this is a matter of morality, coming under the Commandment, "You shall not bear false witness," or among the applications of the standard of truthtelling. But surely no one will argue that it is wicked to believe what facts as you see them force you to believe and wicked to disbelieve what facts as you see them force you to disbelieve.

Actually the matter is more complicated than this. Sin pervades all human actions, including cerebral actions. One of its consequences is that we close our eyes to facts that threaten our positions or threaten beliefs in which we have invested some of our egos; as the proverb noted long ago, "None so blind as those who will not see." On the other hand, we go out of our way to see facts that gratify us. There is also the further complication investigated by the sociology of knowledge. We take on the beliefs of the groups that rear us, or that we join, or that we aspire to being accepted in, such as ethnic communities, economic classes, professional associations, political parties, and religious societies. In each case, these beliefs reflect the biases of the group; they include what the group "would like to believe" because it puts the group in a good light or otherwise serves the group interest. Therefore "facts as one sees them" can be misleading. One can have unconsciously selected the facts that he sees; or one can have had the facts he knows selected for him by the apparatus of his group. Further, one can interpret the facts, or one's group can interpret the facts for him, in a self-serving way. There is even a kind of innocence about this, because one is unconscious of the bias and might even deny its existence if it were pointed out to him. But the bias is there nevertheless.

The application of these considerations to our problem is this: persons can "reject" Jesus (or accept Jesus, for that matter) on the basis of the facts as they see them and still be guilty. Their own self-interest and the self-interest of the groups they belong to can have blinded them to some facts and to the meanings of all the relevant facts. But we do not regard such persons as responsible for their errors for the reason that, unaware of their biases, they have not been free to do better. We can only ask of persons that they act on the facts as they see them after making every effort to see all the relevant ones and to understand them. More we cannot imagine even God demanding. Therefore God cannot be thought of as punishing any Jews past, present, or future as wicked for not believing that Jesus is the Messiah when, for example, they have understood in good faith with Rabbi Akiba that the Messiah must be a "son of David."

5. It is particularly heinous to claim that "the reason the Jews have so much trouble is because God is punishing them. . . ." The Jews really only have "so much trouble" when prejudiced humans visit it upon them. For bigots to call the abuses that they inflict "God's punishments" is, if not to call themselves God, to

blame their viciousness on God in a most self-serving and self-righteous way. Making God the author of their crimes, they powerfully encourage themselves in crime.

6. "The Jews can never be forgiven *for what they did to Jesus. . . .*" These words are not self-explanatory, but back of them lurks the monstrous notion of "deicide," the murdering of God. The allegation, also conveyed in the epithet "Christ-killers," is that "the Jews" murdered the Son of God.

There are two aspects to the shock one sustains in contemplating "deicide." One aspect is the notion of killing God. The other is that "the Jews" are said to have done it. It is not clear from the charge of "deicide" whether it is claimed that the killing was deliberate or inadvertent and whether the killers knew the victim was God or believed it was someone else. But in the absence of any qualifying expressions, it is fair to assume that many have put the most damning construction on "deicide." Thus, there is a people in the world that is so unimaginably evil that they even hate God, the source of all good; they hate God enough to want to kill him; and when the opportunity presented itself to kill the divine Son of God, they eagerly seized it.

How, then, should the story of the Passion of Jesus be told in relation to the Jews? Clearly a familiar way of telling the story has laid an immense burden of guilt on "the Jews," as the Glock and Stark study shows, and has done so in a way that is extremely unfair to Jews. Therefore attention must be given to a manner of telling this most necessary and precious story for the salvation of Christians without doing a monstrous wrong to Jews.

3

PASSION

The New Testament account of the death and resurrection of Jesus functions on two levels. One is the level of history—the other is the level of sacred history. The notion of "sacred history" is one that Jews and Christians share. It is rooted in the belief that the God whom we worship is the Lord of history. God is also the Creator of all things and the Lord of nature. The whole of the natural universe is his handiwork, and he acts in and through all natural processes. But even before God was perceived as the Creator and Lord of nature by the ancient people of Israel, he was recognized as at work in history, operating within historical process to effect the accomplishment of his will.

Perhaps the earliest biblical documentation of this recognition, as Martin Buber suggested, is the Song of Deborah in Judges 5. We have in this song one of the earliest compositions to be found anywhere in the Bible. It is recognizable as such by its being a poem, which suggests that we have it in the same form as that handed on for generations as oral tradition, and by its use of Hebrew words that are archaic in comparison with the vocabulary of the Bible as a whole. It is therefore assigned to the

43

same period—the twelfth century B.C.—as the triumph it celebrates, the victory of a group of Israelite tribes in Canaan over a Canaanite coalition that intended to drive them out. What is most striking about this song of triumph is that the credit for victory is given to Yahweh, the God of Israel. The Canaanite troops had the initiative and superior arms, typified by their chariots, but Yahweh did "march from the region of Edom, the earth trembled, and the heavens dropped, yea the clouds dropped water. The mountains quaked before the Lord, yon Sinai before the Lord, the God of Israel. . . . From heaven fought the stars, from their courses they fought against Sisera. The torrent Kishon swept them away, the onrushing torrent, the torrent Kishon" (Ju. 5:4–5, 20–21). The trembling of the earth in the thunder, the apparent quaking of the mountains in the lightning, the torrents of rain from above, the flooding of the Kishon, all were perceived as the intervention of Yahweh from Sinai, in order to produce the rescue of his people. These perceptions are functions of essentially the same faith that saw the exodus from Egypt as God's act of deliverance of his people and back of that the wanderings of the patriarchs as providentially superintended.

By common consent, the term "history" refers to an account of events that have really happened. "Sacred history," as the term is being used here, is a *kind* of history and therefore is also an account of actual events. But sacred history includes another element, the element of faith in God as the Lord of history. It is therefore an account which sees God playing a role in real events. The eyes of faith are not able to detect God's role in all events, and there is not a sacred history of as many events as are related in history generally. But there are some events that stand out for biblical faith not only as unimaginable without the participation of God but as particularly revealing of the nature of God's will. It is easy to think that the Hebrews who lived through the exodus had little trouble believing that they were the beneficiaries of God's action once they had safely crossed the Yam Suph, the Sea of Reeds, and seen that they were beyond the possibility of being recaptured by the Egyptians. God had been at work in calling and guiding Moses, in helping them to trust and follow Moses, and in the plagues on the Egyptians, in order to bring about a liberation that they could never have won for themselves or even have believed was possible. Thus they believed and they impressed upon their descendants that the exodus was *the type* of God's participation in their history. It established Yahweh as a God of mercy and as their God. "I will redeem you with an outstretched arm and with great acts of judgment, and I will take you for my people, and I will be your God . . ." (Exod. 6:6–7).

Once established in Israel's faith, the belief that God acts in history rooted itself ever more deeply. God was discerned as acting not only in what benefited Israel, like the exodus and the return from the Babylonian captivity, but also in disasters, which were read by the prophets as merited punishments. God was not only recognized in events of the past; he was also counted on to be active in the future, that is, in the hope for a Messiah, according to which God would some day bring in an age of peace, and in the apocalyptic hope that God would terminate all tyranny and oppression. Through Jesus and the apostles the belief that God acts in history became an integral part of Christianity; and in the apostolic preaching the life, death, and resurrection of Jesus are themselves the supreme example of sacred history.

To look at the death of Jesus as sacred history is to see it as an actual historical event and then also as an event in which God can be seen to have been at work. No event can enter into sacred history unless it be an actual historical event. Therefore Christians who want to appropriate what faith sees as saving in Jesus' death need to begin with its actual occurrence. However, it is also true that they will be far more interested in *God's* work in the event than in the details of the human participation, even if it were not true that so many of the latter are difficult to recover.

We begin then with the death of Jesus on the level of ordinary historical occurrence, motivated by ordinary human concerns. First of all, Jesus was one case out of thousands in which Jews of Palestine at the time were treated with abuse, mockery, and execution by the occupying forces of the Roman empire. It was a time of Jewish guerrilla fighters who, like the Maccabean patriots in the years of the Seleucid empire, paid little attention to the odds against them and seized every opportunity to attack Roman garrisons. The guerrilla hope was that God would bless their zeal for freedom, conceived as freedom to follow the Torah, and would hasten the coming of the Messiah. The Messiah in their view was the kind of son of David who would drive out the Romans and crown Jewish independence with the longed-for time of peace and freedom, justice and abundance. Whenever these guerrillas were captured they were *crucified* side by side along the highways as warnings to other Jews who also might have the idea of striking for freedom.

The single most incontrovertible fact about the death of Jesus is that he too was *crucified*. And Jesus' crucifixion is the absolute proof that he was put to death by *Roman* authority. There are many ways in which societies have exacted capital punishment. Romans, and some others but never Jews, used crucifixion, a specially humiliating and torturing manner of execution, for slaves and rebellious subject peoples. The fact that Jesus was crucified under Pontius Pilate means that, however reluctant Pontius Pilate is pictured in the Gospels as having been, he gave the order for Jesus' death.

Generations of Christians have been impressed by the Gospel portrait of a reluctant Pilate wanting to be fair but finally bowing weakly to the pressure of "the Jews." It is striking to compare this conception with the other accounts of Pilate that have survived. He was relieved of his procuratorship in Judea in A.D. 36 because of a reputation for excessive cruelty. Any Roman governor entrusted with responsibility for Roman sovereignty and security in Judea would have been expected to be alert and watchful in regard to insurrectionary movements such as the Zealots and prompt and forceful in putting down rebellion. But even Rome found fault with Pilate for being needlessly provocative, that is, in ordering Roman imperial standards into the city of Jerusalem and in dealing with rising unrest by means of increasing bloodletting. In a letter attributed by Philo to King Agrippa I, who ruled Palestine A.D. 41–44, Pilate is characterized as "unbending and recklessly hard" and his administration is charged with "corruptibility, violence, robberies, ill-treatment of the people, grievances, continuous executions without even the form of a trial, endless and intolerable cruelties."* (Cf. Luke 13:1).

New Testament scholars who have puzzled over these contrasting images of Pilate have made some suggestions. For example, it is important to note that at the time when the Gospels were composed the Christian movement needed the "benign neglect" of the Roman empire in order to exist and carry on its missionary enterprise. It would not have been helpful if Christian documents made it clear that Jesus had been executed as a threat to public order by an official of the empire. Thus, Jesus was crucified "under Pontius Pilate," but not "by the order of" Pilate.

As a result of the same sort of reasoning, it is plain how safe it was, in contrast, to attach the responsibility for pressing for Jesus' death to the office of the high priest, the chief priests, the Sadducean party, and the Sanhedrin. All these institutions had perished in the destruction of Jerusalem in A.D. 70 and were only memories when the Gospels were published.

---

* Emil Schürer, *A History of the Jewish People in the Time of Jesus*, ed. N. N. Glatzer (New York: Schocken, 1961), p. 198.

It is possible that Pilate deliberately gave the appearance of being reluctant to crucify Jesus in order to make it clear for the record how urgently the high priest and his supporters were demanding Jesus' death. In that way he would be able to say if he were ever challenged that he had been anything but harsh and cruel—the vindictiveness was all in Jesus' own people. On this view, Pilate was taking advantage of the high priest's demands but was still serving his own purposes in executing Jesus. For a Roman procurator would know that the Jews were serious about recovering their freedom, that the Passover season —commemoration of the exodus—was a time when liberation was very much on their minds, and that any Messianic move- ment was by definition a threat to Roman rule in Judea. He would have had his undercover agents on the alert especially at Passover for any such signs as the Hosannas ("Salvation Now!") that the crowds shouted to Jesus when he entered Jerusalem on the Sunday before his arrest. Any Roman governor of Judea, and especially one known for cruelty, would never have taken any chances or waited too long to act in the face of a Messianic movement. Therefore, it was both in the nature of his office and in character for Pilate to order Jesus' crucifixion. In any case, it was necessary for the Roman procurator to give the authorization for Jesus to have been crucified.

What then was the role of Jews in the death of Jesus?

Jews who lived before or after Jesus' ministry had absolutely nothing to do with Jesus' death. If there have been 150 genera- tions of Jews since Abraham, the Jews who lived before or after Jesus constitute more than 99 percent of all Jews.

Jews who were alive in Jesus' time but lived *outside* Judea and Galilee had nothing to do with Jesus' death, and they were the vast majority of Jews alive in Jesus' time by a factor of about six to one.

Of the Jews who lived in Galilee and Judea in Jesus' time, how many heard of him and of these how many made any kind of response such as going somewhere to see and hear him? There is no way to know. What the Gospels suggest, however, is that people who did encounter him heard him gladly. As many as five thousand at a time gathered to see and hear him and stayed with him by the hour, forgetting about mealtimes. When he taught in the temple courtyard during the last week of his life, the crowds around him were so large and so much attached to him that the temple police did not dare to arrest him (Luke 19:45–48). Who were these friendly crowds? Except for an occasional Roman soldier, they were Jews.

Did Jesus have opposition and enemies, too, among his fellow Jews? He had both. Some of the Pharisees answer the description of opposition. They differed with Jesus chiefly with regard to the divine law. When Jesus' disciples plucked grain as they walked on the Sabbath, "threshed" it in their hands, and ate it, it was Pharisees who challenged Jesus' permissiveness (Mark 2:24). The disciples were seen as in violation of the Pharisees' strict interpretation of the biblical prohibition of work on the Sabbath. When Jesus asked in a synagogue if it was permitted to heal a man with a withered arm on the Sabbath, what Jesus asked, according to Mark, was whether it was "lawful on the Sabbath to do good or to do harm, to save life or to kill" (Mark 3:4), suggesting that not to heal when the opportunity arose was to do harm. The Pharisees took offense when Jesus healed the man. For the Pharisees it was lawful to expend effort such as was normally prohibited on the Sabbath provided it was necessary to save life; but presumably the man with the withered arm was not in danger of death and could have waited for treatment until the Sabbath was ended. It was scribes of the Pharisees who were upset when Jesus ate with tax collectors and other such sinners (Mark 2:16). The Pharisees questioned the fact that Jesus' disciples ate with unwashed hands in violation of "the tradition of the elders." This tradition was the oral law that the Pharisees and their predecessors had developed and were developing as interpretation and application of the biblical laws; thus they provoked Jesus' attack on the "tradition."

And he said to them, "You have a fine way of rejecting the commandment of God, in order to keep your tradition! For Moses said, 'Honor your father and mother'; and, 'He who speaks evil of father or mother, let him surely die'; but you say, 'If a man tells his father or his mother, What you would have gained from me is Corban' (that is, given to God)—then you no longer permit him to do anything for his father or mother, thus making void the word of God through your tradition which you hand on. . . ." (Mark 7:1–13)

There are perhaps two separate issues of disagreement in these episodes. One is the validity of the whole enterprise of developing the oral law. The other is the wisdom or appropriateness of any particular item within the oral law such as the Corban rule or any of the Sabbath rules.

What is clearest in the controversy between Jesus and the Pharisees is their difference about specific items in the oral law or tradition of the elders, such as the Corban rule. What may need to be made clearer for Christians is that such Pharisee positions were arrived at and taught in good faith. In the case of the Corban rule, the Pharisees were no doubt defending the sanctity of vows made to God. Such a vow, promising to God what might have gone toward the support of elderly parents, could have been made unwisely, that is, in the heat of temporary irritation with the parents. Nevertheless, the Pharisees were insisting, it was a vow made to God. It is also noteworthy that such Pharisee positions were arrived at in their academies by a democratic process. Innovations were debated at great length and adopted by majority vote of the teachers of the law. Furthermore they were always subject to modification by subsequent majorities. Thus, the Corban rule that was in effect in Jesus' day was modified by the time the oral law was codified in the Mishnah (c. A.D. 200) in such a way as to safeguard the rights of parents.

What Jesus was concerned for in these episodes was that human traditions should not be permitted to defeat the humane intention of God's law, that is, that the poor shall eat and the handicapped be healed.

As to the validity of the whole enterprise of developing the oral law, the differences between Jesus and the Pharisees are not so clear. That is, did Jesus deplore the very idea of having the oral law?

If the oral law as the Pharisees developed it is seen as *interpretation* of the law of God as given in the scriptures, it is not at all established that Jesus was opposed to oral law as such. On the contrary, it can be argued that Jesus himself founded his own tradition of "oral law." The Sermon on the Mount is full of instances in which Jesus took up items from the law of Moses and interpreted them. In some cases his interpretation made the law of Moses more demanding by requiring obedience to it even at the level of impulse: "You have heard that it was said, 'You shall not commit adultery.' But I say to you that every one who looks at a woman lustfully has already committed adultery with her in his heart" (Matt. 5:27–28). In other cases, Jesus is pictured as interpreting the Mosaic law in such a way as to change what it called for in overt behavior: "It was also said, 'Whoever divorces his wife, let him give her a certificate of divorce.' But I say to you that everyone who divorces his wife, except on the ground of unchastity, makes her an adulteress; and whoever marries a divorced woman commits adultery" (Matt. 5:31–32). It is even clear, in the Gospel of Matthew at least, that Jesus founded a kind of "Christian scribism" and authorized the apostles too to tighten and loosen the requirements of the law: "Truly, I say to you, whatever you bind on earth shall be bound in heaven, and whatever you loose on earth shall be loosed in heaven" (Matt. 18:18). Rabbinic usage contemporaneous with

Jesus shows that to bind and to loose meant to forbid and to permit various kinds of behavior in view of the law of God. Jesus was, as the Gospel of Matthew saw him, a rabbi and not radically different from the Pharisees.

However that may be, the Pharisees clearly operated in good faith. No society can function without some provision for updating its laws. Times change. Old regulations become irrelevant or impossible and new formulas are required; new problems arise and new applications of the basic law are called for. The collection of biblical law in the so-called books of Moses was at least four hundred years old in Jesus' day. There had to be some ongoing arrangement for interpreting the intentions back of the biblical law in relation to the realities of the present. According to Mishnaic tradition, there had never been a time when such an arrangement did not exist: Moses himself had received the whole Torah, both written *and oral*, at Mount Sinai, and it had been handed down from generation to generation, Moses to Joshua, Joshua to the elders, the elders to the prophets, and the prophets to the men of the Great Assembly. The Pharisees saw themselves—or at any rate their teachers—as the successors of the men of the Great Assembly. As they saw it, even when they innovated, they were doing nothing more than to make explicit what was already implicit in the tradition. The development of the Sabbath law, from its biblical simplicity to its ultimate elaborateness, is a case in point.

It is obvious that Jews themselves do not agree today about the authority of this oral law—which finally became *written* law and is the heart of the Talmud. The major difference between traditionalist and modernist Jews has to do with whether these laws are still relevant and still in effect as God's laws and, if not all of them are, which ones are. What cannot be doubted, however, is that it is the rich legal tradition of the Talmud that has determined Jewish character and culture down to modern times. What was once said of the Sabbath can as well be said about the

Talmudic law. Ahad Ha-Am (Asher Ginzberg, 1856–1927) once observed that "more than the Jews have kept the Sabbath, the Sabbath has kept the Jews";* that is, the Sabbath has kept the Jews Jews, has been their bulwark against assimilation and loss of moral and spiritual identity. So likewise more than the Jews have kept the Talmud, the Talmud has kept the Jews. The point is that the Talmud is the legacy of the Pharisee party.

What we have between Jesus and the Pharisees, then, are differences as to how the biblical law was to be interpreted and applied and possibly further differences as to how explicit and formal and rigid the legal tradition as a whole was to be allowed to become. These are matters about which honest persons can differ and differ sharply, and strong-minded persons argue *invincibly*, and on the basis of which some may want to sever ties of fellowship. But in a pluralistic Jewish religious world they were not matters to be resolved by force or bloodshed. Thus, the Pharisees can be identified as opponents of Jesus, but not as enemies. Entirely consistent with this, the Synoptic Gospels assign no role whatsoever to the Pharisees in the plotting that led to Jesus' death. That this must have been the way it was in Jesus' experience is also indicated by the experiences of the apostles, as reported by the book of Acts, when they preached the good news of the resurrection in Jerusalem; their antagonists were "the priests and the captain of the temple, and the Sadducees" (Acts 4:1; cf. 5:17).

The typical Pharisee attitude is indicated by the rabbinical teacher Gamaliel as he is depicted in the book of Acts (Acts 5:33–39) saying, "If this plan or this undertaking [the Christian proclamation] is of men, it will fail; but if it is of God, you will not be able to overthrow them. You might even be found opposing God!"

Since Jews today are the disciples of the Pharisees in approxi-

*Nathan Ausubel, *The Book of Jewish Knowledge* (New York: Crown Publishers, Inc., 1964), p. 374a.

mately the same sense as Christians are disciples of Jesus, something more ought to be said about the Pharisees. There is no doubt that they have received a bad reputation among Christians —the use of the adjective "pharisaic" as a synonym for "hypocritical" is symbolic of this. This usage owes a great deal to an address by Jesus reported in Matthew 23, the refrain of which is "Woe to you, scribes and Pharisees, hypocrites." Seen in its historical context, this address by Jesus is another instance of prophetic Jewish self-criticism. The Talmud itself, the ultimate product of the oral tradition that the Pharisees were then developing, includes a similar passage in which various types of Pharisees are condemned. The nearest analogy to these judgments on the Pharisees by Jesus and in the Talmud is a Christian sermon in which the typical sins of churchgoers are condemned. We Christians promise better than we perform, we pretend to be better than we are, given our commitment to the imitation of Jesus we are failures, etc. What any Christian would immediately resent is the taking of such a sermon by a representative of another religion and concluding from it that the Christians were the villains of the world. It would be just as absurd to conclude from the remarks of Jesus and the Talmud that the Pharisees were the villains of the Jewish world. On the contrary, they were a movement of reform. They were critical of Jesus and he was critical of them precisely because they stood close to each other and had so much in common, especially their common intention to call their people to doing the will of God.

If Jesus did have Jewish enemies, they will be found among the Sadducees and the chief priests and the Sanhedrin. But curiously, this enmity had less to do with religion than with politics. It is true that Jesus and the Sadducees were poles apart on some religious questions. The one example given in all three Synoptic Gospels is the question of the resurrection. The Sadducees did not believe in it because, according to their understanding, it was not taught in the five books of Moses, and these were the only books that they accepted as holy scripture. They asked Jesus a question that was intended to ridicule the resurrection (about seven brothers married successively to one woman—in the resurrection whose wife will she be?) but Jesus met them on their own ground and gave them an argument for the resurrection based on the book of Exodus (Mark 12:18–27). Nevertheless, the Sadducean enmity toward Jesus was essentially political and practical.

The Sadducees were a Jewish party made up of aristocratic, wealthy, and priestly families who reflected the interests of the temple and the point of view of the high priest. The high priest was the highest-ranking Jewish person not only cultically—he presided over all temple affairs and he alone entered the Holy of Holies once a year on the Day of Atonement (*Yom Kippur*) —but also politically—he was responsible to the Roman imperial government for law and order. (Guerrilla warfare against the Romans, such as that waged by the Zealots, was irregular and unofficial as far as Jewish society as a whole was concerned and the Romans dealt with it directly.) A hundred years before Jesus' ministry, the incumbent high priest was also the king of an independent Jewish state in Palestine, and some of the former pomp still clung to the high priest's office.

Jesus must have made himself very offensive in the sight of the high priest and his party on the occasion referred to as "the cleansing of the temple." Jesus overthrew the tables of the money-changers and the seats of those who sold pigeons and he drove out those who bought and sold in the temple and he said: "Is it not written, 'My house shall be called a house of prayer for all the nations'? But you have made it a den of robbers" (Mark 11:17).

Jesus engaged here in what we have become accustomed to call a "demonstration." It was an acted-out protest against the extortion practiced by the temple establishment. For one thing, animals offered to the priesthood for sacrifice, from pigeons on

up to the most expensive animals, had to be "unblemished."
The ones who judged the animals were the priests. If the priests
rejected anyone's animal, there was only one way to proceed
with the required sacrifice, and that was to buy a certified
animal from the priests. The law that required an "unblemished" animal expressed the judgment that only the best sort of
offering was fit to be presented to the Lord. But the opening for
corruption is obvious when one considers that to have one's
animal rejected was to be compelled to purchase a fit animal
from the priests, which gave the temple a monopoly and the
price structure that goes with monopoly. The temple operated
another monopoly. In order to purchase an animal, a pilgrim
had to pay with temple currency. That meant purchasing temple
money, again at monopolistic prices, from the temple money-
changers. No wonder Jesus called the temple a "den of robbers"
and made as vigorous a protest as he did. His pious, law-observ-
ing fellow-countrymen were being subjected to extortion precisely on the ground of their piety and by institutionalized religion itself in what was supposed to be God's house.

Jesus was not alone in feeling as he did about the temple
administration. The temple had been losing favor with the
common people for generations already; it was perpetuated
chiefly because biblical law specified that worship had to be per-
formed in it. Shortly after (A.D. 70) not only was Judaism to
lose it when the Romans destroyed it, but Jews were to do without it very well. Thus when Jesus expressed his judgment as
strongly and publicly as he did, given his prestige and popular-
ity, the temple administration was bound to be threatened and
shaken. This alone could have motivated some chief priests to
seek "a way to destroy him" (Mark 11:18).

But the high priest's chief reason to fear Jesus and to want to
be rid of him centered on Jesus' connection with Messiahship. It
is not clear what kind of hopes the Sadducees themselves enter-
tained with reference to the Messiah. Since the Messiah was not

spoken of in the books of Moses, they may have been totally uncommitted to any expectation of a Messiah. But they were bound to know that most of their fellow-countrymen were eagerly looking forward to the coming of the Messiah and that the Messiah's coming was expected to bring an end to the Roman occupation. They therefore knew that the Romans would inevitably, in defense of their military and political position in the Middle East, take a most serious view of any Messianic movement and endeavor to crush it.

It is not even a certainty that the Sadducees would have welcomed a successful eviction of the Romans from Palestine. They were more dependent on the Romans for their wealth and status than they were on their fellow-Jews. They were not popular with Jews generally. They were exploiters of their own people. They were rich in a poor land where most families were poor. They would hardly have been trusted with power by a self-determining Jewish population. On the other hand, they were useful to the Romans by providing a show of Jewish self-rule in Palestine, and the Romans rewarded their collaboration by keeping them in office and in possession of their wealth and of their access to wealth. Therefore the Sadducees had good reason to fear any Messianic movement, even one with the best prospects for success.

How much more they must have feared *incipient* Messianic movements, with dim or uncertain hopes of success! Such movements could only unleash full-scale war in which they could expect no quarter from either the Romans or their fellow-Jews. What they had to fear in Jesus' time was subsequently spelled out in historical events that developed in the war of A.D. 66–70. A Jewish freedom movement succeeded at the beginning in inflicting heavy losses on the Roman troops and in liberating most of Judea and Galilee. But Rome brought in powerful armies and relentlessly reduced each Jewish stronghold in turn and slaughtered its defenders. Before Jerusalem finally fell,

Jewish rebels murdered one high priest and deposed another to replace him with one of their own party. In the final destruction, the temple as well as the city was totally wrecked, and the whole priesthood and the Sadducean party disappeared.

It is in the light of Sadducean fears of Messianic movements that one understands the Sadducees' response to Jesus. He was not only a teacher with whose views they were out of sympathy, and he was not only a dangerous because popular critic of their administration of the temple. He was a man identified somehow in the minds of many with the coming of the Messiah. The "triumphant entry" of Jesus into Jerusalem that Christians commemorate on Palm Sunday was the kind of signal that the Roman police and the temple police (those in the service of the high priest) would have been looking for and would have reported nervously. For the crowd that greeted Jesus called out, "Hosanna! Blessed is he who comes in the name of the Lord! Blessed is the kingdom of our father David that is coming! Hosanna in the highest!" (Mark 11:9–10). "Hosanna" is based on the Hebrew for a prayer calling upon God to save : "O save!" or "Give salvation now!" In the triumphal entry Jesus was clearly pointed to as the occasion of a Messianic demonstration; and he naturally became identified as an important revolutionist.

It is clear to us that the Gospel-writers do not at all see Jesus as interested in a political rebellion against Rome. However, given what the term "Messiah" meant to most people in Jerusalem at the time, it is not surprising that both the Sadducees and the Romans should have reacted with alarm against anyone who generated Messianic salutations and invocations (Hosanna!). Thus, as we should expect and the Gospels indicate, Jesus was arrested by the temple police, under the authority of the high priest, and was brought to a hearing before the high priest and his aides and councillors (members of the Sanhedrin) who investigated his relation to the Messiahship (Mark 14:43, 53,

61–62). Whether the chief priests really believed that it was blasphemous for Jesus to speak about his Messiahship and the coming of the Son of Man, as the Synoptic Gospels claim—and it is not clear how this could be construed as blasphemy—it is nevertheless the testimony of all four Gospels that the high priest and his councillors delivered Jesus to Pilate for the purpose of having him executed; also that the charge against Jesus before Pilate was the political charge of insurrection—"King of the Jews." This action is interpreted by the remark attributed to the high priest in John's Gospel, "that it was expedient that one man should die for the people" (John 18:14). That is, whether or not the prisoner Jesus was guilty of leading an insurrectionary movement against the Romans, if the people *believed* that he was and struck for freedom in his name, then it was bound to be war, and that could not go well for the (Jewish) people. It was better that one man should die than the whole people.

Judas was not an important factor in the effort to get rid of Jesus; but his role was dramatic and memorable and his story may be specially productive of hostile Christian images of "the Jew."

Judas was described by the Gospels as contracting with the chief priests to "betray" Jesus. What Judas had to sell was an insider's information as to where Jesus would be after dark, when he would no longer be surrounded by enthusiastic crowds of listeners. This was useful to persons who intended to arrest Jesus and wished to do so with the minimum of publicity and resistance. However, if Judas had not volunteered, the same information could have been acquired from an informer concealed among the disciples or from someone hired to shadow Jesus.

What an arch-villain Judas appears to be, however, when he steps forward for the betrayer's role from within the inner circle of apostles! Someone whom Jesus trusted that much and for whom he had such high expectations turned him over to his enemies for money! And the one who stabbed his friend in the back for money carried the name Judas, that is, Judah, the very name of the Jewish nation.

It may be, as Richard Rubinstein has suggested, that the Judas story is the most damaging single item among Christians' negative associations with Jews. At any rate it is clear that Christians identify Judas as a Jew. According to the Glock and Stark study, more than five times as many Protestants recognize Peter, Paul, and the other apostles as Christians as recognize them as Jews. But when it comes to Judas, almost twice as many Christians identify him as a Jew as identify him as a Christian.*

What can be said to place the story of Judas in a truer perspective? It has already been pointed out that Judas did not play an important role and certainly not a necessary role in bringing about Jesus' death. If Judas had not come forward, Jesus would still have been arrested and crucified. In addition, large numbers of readers of the story of Jesus have been left unconvinced by the portrayal of Judas betraying Jesus for thirty pieces of silver. It is hard to believe that someone Jesus picked as an apostle could have been motivated in that way. Hence it has been speculated that Judas acted in an effort to force Jesus to be more militant. Perhaps he thought that if Jesus were threatened with death he would be forced to take up the role of son of David and drive the Romans out of the land. Perhaps he thought that if Jesus were unable to do that he would then be exposed as not the real Messiah. Suggestions such as these are speculative. Their value is that they show the possibility that Judas, far from having to be a model of pure wickedness, can be seen to be like the other figures in the Passion drama—a model of human fallibility.

Thus far we have been considering the death of Jesus as *his-*

*Charles Y. Glock and Rodney Stark, *Christian Beliefs and Anti-Semitism* (New York: Harper & Row, 1966), pp. 47–49.

tory, as a product of the same sort of human interaction that constitutes any event. On this plane, one can investigate the roles of various groups or interests in Jesus' time and place, such as Pontius Pilate, the group around him including soldiers, and the Roman imperial interests they served, and such a group as the Sadducees and the interests that held them together. But the story of the death of Jesus has its real value to the Christian community as a part of *sacred history*. Jesus' death is seen as part of a great drama that is as precious as it is because in it God reveals himself. God is seen by the eye of faith as one who loves his children to the point of self-sacrifice, who pities his children in the miseries their sins have drawn upon them, and who provides a way by which the sins of all of them may be forgiven and overcome. "God was in Christ reconciling the world to himself . . ." (2 Cor. 5:19).

The Hebrew Bible was ransacked in New Testament times for figures and examples by which the reconciling work of God in Jesus could be grasped and explained. Jesus was the "paschal (Passover) lamb" (1 Cor. 5:7) who had been sacrificed. That is, a lamb had been sacrificed at the exodus so that its blood might be applied to the lintel and doorposts and the angel of death thereby warned away from the Hebrew homes and directed to the Egyptian homes, and the liberation from Egypt was thereby made possible; just so Jesus had been sacrificed at Passover time and liberation from sin and guilt had been made possible.

"But when Christ appeared as a high priest of the good things that have come, . . . he entered once for all into the Holy Place, taking not the blood of goats and calves but his own blood, thus securing an eternal redemption" (Heb. 9:11–12; see Hebrews 9 in its entirety). Here the author of the Epistle to the Hebrews likens Jesus to the Jewish high priest, who regularly made a sacrifice of the blood of animals for the purification of his people. But Christ sacrificed his own blood, and thus brought a sacrifice on behalf of sinners that need not be repeated, but is effective for all time.

Jesus himself at the Last Supper speaks of "the new covenant in my blood" (1 Cor. 11:25). Thus, just as the original covenant was sealed at Sinai when Moses sprinkled blood on the altar and on the people (Exod. 24:5–8), so the new covenant with God, open to all mankind, is sealed and made valid by the blood of Christ.

Jesus is also seen (e.g., in 1 Pet. 2:24–25) as the suffering servant of the Lord described in Isaiah 53, who "was despised and rejected by men." But, "surely he has borne our griefs and carried our sorrows; . . . he was wounded for our transgressions, he was bruised for our iniquities; upon him was the chastisement that made us whole, and with his stripes we are healed. . . . the Lord has laid on him the iniquity of us all" (Isa. 53:3–6). "It was the will of the Lord to bruise him; . . . [and] the will of the Lord shall prosper in his hand" (Isa. 53:10). In all this "the arm of the Lord [has] been revealed" (Isa. 53:1).

Sacred history is the story of God in his dealings with humanity. By the same token, it is the story of humanity in relation to God. But what is striking in these typical New Testament passages in which *sacred* history is being pointed to and its meaning explicated is that the particular guilt of Pilate and of the Sadducees and others drops out of sight, and the guilt involved in the unjust execution of Jesus is generalized to all humanity, but especially to the Christians. "He himself bore *our* sins in his body on the tree, that *we* might die to sin and live to righteousness" (1 Pet. 2:24; italics mine).

The uncomfortable side of this truth is that all persons, specifically all Christians, can be identified as the crucifiers. That is, the sins of the original crucifiers that led them to be crucifiers are present in us. Therefore, we are more or less interchangeable with them. We can see ourselves in them. This is because sin is universal, because it is ruthless pursuit of what we take to be our own interests, and because sin is capable of anything, given the conducive circumstances. This has been the burden of centuries of sound Lenten preaching. Judas betrayed him—what betrayals are we engaged in? Peter denied him, the disciples fled and abandoned him, the Sadducees conspired against him because he threatened their self-interest. Herod mocked him. Pilate sentenced him. The soldiers callously killed him. What denials, abandonments, conspiracies, mockings, unjust sentencings, callousness are we engaged in?

The comforting side of the same truth is that the crucifiers are forgiven. God was in Christ praying, "Father, forgive them; for they know not what they do" (Luke 23:34). The sacred history, after sweeping all of us into the collection of the guilty, pronounces to all of us the absolution. No wonder the sacred history is precious. It is our fundamental assurance that we will never be beyond the reach of God's forgiveness. Therefore we need never despair. At the same time, all who experience the absolution under the cross are also persons who have been sensitized to the devilish consequences that flow from our ordinary sinfulness—who see that nothing less than the crucifixion is entailed. Thus they are also persons in whom the spirit of God is at work healing them of their ruthless self-concern and winning them over to the way of love.

It is appropriate to history *as such* that names be named—Pharisees, Judas, Peter, Annas and Caiaphas (high priests), Sadducees, Herod, Pilate. It is appropriate to *sacred* history that it be perceived as real history. Therefore we cannot wish these names out of the Gospel accounts of Jesus' death. But it is a fact that the roles played by some of these persons and groups in the Gospel story have fed into antisemitism. What shall be done? Two things, at least. Whenever the story of Jesus' death is read in the church, or preached on, or studied in church schools, (1) the real roles of Pharisees, scribes, Sadducees, and priests can be clarified, in good faith, so that the presumption of their good faith can be appreciated as valid; (2) the point can be stressed that all who stood among the crucifiers are stand-ins for us. They are paradigms of ourselves whose highest role is to make us aware of our own guilt and of our own access to forgiveness.

4

HOLOCAUST

"Holocaust" refers originally to a sacrificial offering in which the whole carcass is consumed by fire—typically the "whole burnt offering" commanded in Leviticus 4 as an expiation for unwitting sin. "Holocaust" has become the standard term by which Jews and others refer to the murder of six million Jews by the Nazis in 1939–1945.

No words are adequate either for describing or for condemning this most unimaginable crime, compounded of six million crimes of murder. All the terrors, indignities, and tortures visited upon Jews from the days of Antiochus Epiphanes down through all the Christian centuries were added up, quadrupled, and then visited upon one generation in the holocaust. Never before was a murderous attack on an indigenous minority conducted for so long, so widely, and so *efficiently*. The explicit goal was to eliminate every Jew from the human race, so that there could never again be any Jews, and then to eliminate all records and relics of Jewish life, so that the world would be as though there never had been any Jews.

In earlier generations, Jews had frequently been told, "You are not to live among us as Jews." That meant, if you are going to insist on living among us, you may not do so as Jews. Be baptized! So it was in Spain in 1391. Or, the meaning was, if you are going to insist on continuing to be Jews, you may not live among us. Be gone! So it was in England in 1290, in Spain in 1492. But under the Nazi regime the Jews were told, "You are not to live." Deportation of Jews was not enough for the Nazis. Wherever Jews would live they would be a corruption of a world the Nazis proposed to inherit. Jews were simply not to survive.

What does the holocaust mean? What does it mean to Jews? What to Christians? The answer is not necessarily a verbal formula about human nature or even about antisemitism. As we shall see, not all Jews learn the same lessons from the holocaust. But one thing in this area that Jews do seem to agree about is that they want Christians to join with them in working on the problem of understanding the holocaust. Considering the involvement of Christians in the existence of antisemitism, how can we do less? We may not simply act as if nothing has happened.

Because six million torture-murders are simply unimaginable, it is a requirement for Christians to read such a book as Elie Wiesel's *Night*,* in which the focus is on one family, Wiesel's own, from the first warnings about "resettlement" that threatened their little Transylvanian town in 1944 until a year later when his mother, father, and three sisters were dead. Elie was fifteen when all the Jews in the town were crowded into two ghettos, stripped of all their possessions, and then marched to the railway station to be crowded into cattle cars.

When they arrived at Auschwitz (of which none of them had heard), they were greeted by the sickening smell of burning flesh. Males and females were brusquely separated with no time for leave-taking, and Elie (and his father) never saw or heard

*Elie Wiesel, *Night* (New York: Hill and Wang, 1960).

of his mother and sisters again. One of the first things Elie saw in the camp was a truckload of children's corpses being dumped into a pit of fire. The very young and the old were selected at once for the gas chambers; the able-bodied were spared to be worked to death. Elie and his father were repeatedly beaten. The whole camp was forced to watch the hangings of the worst offenders.

One day the hanging was of two men and a boy. The boy's body was so light that his neck was not broken in the fall. For a half hour he slowly choked to death. Someone behind Elie asked, "Where is God now?" And Elie heard a voice within him answer, "Here he is—He is hanging here on this gallows" (p. 71).

In one way, this saying proclaims the suffering God who is not safe in heaven, but dwells among us, even within us, and feels all the pains and all the dying of all of us. In another way, what is proclaimed is the "death of God," the judgment that so much unchecked cruelty makes a mockery of the idea of a Father who cares. Thus faith is murdered, and God is murdered, as Wiesel says elsewhere when he speaks of "moments which murdered my God and my soul" (p. 44). A few weeks before, young Elie had been a Hasid, who lived for nothing but to study Torah. But a Messiah who could have come and yet did not come at Auschwitz—what is one to believe about him?

Elie noted, too, how dehumanizing the whole camp process was for all the prisoners, how the brutality and the starvation could reduce a son to fighting his own father for possession of a crust of bread.

Elie's father finally sickened, became delirious, could not understand a guard's order, and was beaten to death. Elie survived three months more, until the camp was liberated in April, 1945. Today he continues to write mostly about the holocaust. He does not tell us what it means. He simply goes on asking Jews and gentiles alike to *remember*.

Emil Fackenheim, a Jewish philosopher and theologian, agrees with Wiesel in seeing the event of the death camps as somehow as momentous and revelatory as the event at Mount Sinai. He believes that at least one new commandment is addressed to Jews from this Sinai:

Jews are not permitted to hand Hitler posthumous victories. Jews are commanded to survive as Jews, lest their people perish. They are commanded to remember the victims of Auschwitz, lest their memory perish. They are forbidden to despair of God, lest Judaism perish. They are forbidden to despair of the world as the domain of God, lest the world be handed over to the forces of Auschwitz. For a Jew to break this commandment would be to do the unthinkable—to respond to Hitler by doing his work.*

Another Jewish thinker who has struggled to deal with the murder of the six million is Rabbi Richard Rubinstein, the author of *After Auschwitz.*† Rubinstein tells a story of a conversation he had in 1961 with Dean Heinrich Grüber of the Evangelical Church in Berlin. Grüber was recognized after World War II as one of the Christian heroes of the Nazi period. He risked his life and his family's safety by denouncing the attacks on Jews and by intervening to provide ways of escape from Europe for as many Jews as he could. He was sent to Dachau concentration camp and nearly lost his life there. In his conversation with Rubinstein, Grüber is pictured as understanding the holocaust in what Rubinstein refers to as "Deuteronomist" terms, that is, in the manner of the book of Deuteronomy and of the prophets of Israel. God is the Lord of history. When Israel is obedient to the commandments of the Lord, it is well with her. When disaster falls upon Israel, it is because God is punishing her for disobedience.

Isaiah presents God as speaking of Assyria as "the rod of my

*Emil Fackenheim, *Quest for Past and Future* (Bloomington: Indiana University Press, 1968), p. 20.
†Richard L. Rubinstein, *After Auschwitz* (New York: Bobbs-Merrill, 1966).

anger" (Isa. 10:5). The destruction and military defeat that Assyria brought upon Israel in the eighth century B.C. was really God's action. That was not to say, however, that Assyria was thereby vindicated. It was acting out its own dreams of empire, for its own aggrandizement and not for the sake of God. In fact, Assyria believed that it had humiliated the God of Israel as well as Israel itself. Not so, said Isaiah. "Shall the axe vaunt itself over him who hews with it . . .?" (Isa. 10:15). Once Assyria has served God's purpose, it will be punished in turn. "The Lord will destroy, both soul and body, and it will be [for Assyria] as when a sick man wastes away" (Isa. 10:18).

Grüber is reported as applying this line of thought to the holocaust. Hitler is interchangeable with Assyria, or with Nebuchadnezzar, the Babylonian king who destroyed Jerusalem and the temple in 586 B.C. The destructive action is really God's action. The cause of God's action is the sins of the Jews. (What sins? Grüber does not say, but Rubinstein suspects that it is, once again, the sin of rejecting Jesus as the Messiah.) This does not vindicate Hitler, in Grüber's view, any more than Isaiah saw Assyria as vindicated. Hitler was motivated by his own arrogant imperialist dreams as well as by hatred of the God of Jews and Christians. Therefore the wrath of God also descended on Hitler and on the German people in the course of World War II, and rightly so, in Grüber's view.

Rubinstein is appalled. This is, for him, the reduction to absurdity of the whole idea of the God of history and of sacred history. "If there is a God of history, he is the ultimate author of Auschwitz" (*After Auschwitz*, p. 204). Therefore, there is no God of history. The only alternative to the Deuteronomist view of history is the view that human suffering and indeed the whole world itself are meaningless. This is Rubinstein's conclusion. The death camps are the end of the God of history and of the "chosenness" of the chosen people. From now on Jews must expect nothing from history but perpetual alienation. The only

Messiah is death. Death is the only resolution of conflict, insecurity, and alienation. It is time to invoke again the old gods of nature who supply the grain and the flax, the oil and the wine, as in the days of Canaan. One can celebrate the finite joys of human life in the framework of Jewish law and Jewish liturgy. But the Lord of history disappears into a God who is the "Holy Nothingness" out of which all things came and to which all things return.

It is important to note that Rubinstein is not typical of Jews. An eloquent and a captivating voice he has, but not a significant Jewish following. His solution to the problem of understanding the holocaust is radical and evidently too radical to be recognizably Jewish to Jews. It is a solution of the holocaust at the price of the dissolution of Jewish faith. But what it really puts before us is a glimpse of the agony of contemplating the holocaust. If one permits oneself to look intently at the holocaust, there is the risk that one will be changed. Rubinstein mentions Jews who have felt forced to conclude that Judaism is *not worth saving* at the cost entailed in the suffering and death that will be visited on sons and daughters, grandsons and granddaughters, for being born Jewish.

Is Rubinstein right in seeing no third possibility beyond agreeing with the Deuteronomist that suffering proves guilt, on the one hand, or deciding on the other hand that history is meaningless? The Bible itself is witness that the Deuteronomist's view was too simple for some ancient persons of the biblical faith. Habakkuk the prophet challenged it. "Why," he prayed to God in the face of Babylonian threats of invasion, "dost thou look on faithless men, and art silent when the wicked swallows up the man more righteous than he?" (Hab. 1:13). No justification of God's ways was offered to Habakkuk, and he developed no theoretical answer of his own. His solution: *trust* in God in spite of not understanding. "The righteous shall live by his faith" (Hab. 2:4). The appeal to his fellows for faith in spite of appearances is a clear rejection of the Deuteronomist doctrine.

The book of Job, which is usually read as a study of the problem of the suffering of the righteous *individual*, can also be read as focused on Habakkuk's problem. "Job" may be the people Israel. Job does not claim to be perfect, any more than Habakkuk claims that the people Israel is perfect. The complaint is, why is the suffering out of all proportion to the seriousness of the offenses committed? Is God really just? Why is the relatively innocent nation or person afflicted with calamities that only the most wicked could deserve? Job's question also elicits no clear doctrinal reply. Thus the book of Job, also, seems to call for *faith* that God knows what he is doing and that we can live without an answer as long as we trust God. Even more than Habakkuk, Job strenuously rebuts the Deuteronomist idea that suffering proves guilt.

Jesus, too, rejected the Deuteronomist teaching.

There were some present at that very time who told him of the Galileans whose blood Pilate had mingled with their sacrifices. And he answered them, "Do you think that these Galileans were worse sinners than all the other Galileans, because they suffered thus? I tell you, No; but unless you repent, you will all likewise perish." (Luke 13:1–3)

Suffering does occur as punishment for sin; but the fact of one's suffering does not establish the fact of one's equivalent sin, because there are *other* causes of suffering besides one's own sin —such as others' sins.

The biblical challenge to the Deuteronomist formula for God's governance suggests that there must be a way to hold to sacred history and to the God of history without being Deuteronomist.

Augustine taught that God works in all processes and acts in all events. Thus there can be "sacred history," that is, a way of perceiving some events, at least, in such a way as to discern

God's action within them. But this is not to say that God *alone* acts in all events, which would be to say that God is the sole cause of all that happens, and that whatever happens is the will of God. Therefore no particular event or complex of events, and certainly not the holocaust, is required for those who believe in the God of history to be an act of God. The events of history are the extremely complicated resultants of the acts of all free wills—God's acts plus the acts of all human beings. There are human beings, like Moses and Jesus as sacred history sees them, who are inspired by God and whose actions are the actions of God. There are human beings, like Nebuchadnezzar as Jeremiah saw him, who are self-serving and who yet are rods of God's anger. (But there is no logical requirement to say of Hitler what may be true of Nebuchadnezzar.) There are human beings, like Pilate as Jesus saw him and like Hitler, whose wills are opposed to the will of God, who work at cross-purposes with God, and who counteract and negate the benevolent will of God in given events.

William James invented an image that expresses essentially this same view of history. James envisioned history as mankind seated at one end of a chessboard and God at the other. The moves that humanity makes are chosen by humanity. God has no control of them. Humanity's moves are the resultants of many individual moves, some supportive of others, some quite at cross-purposes with others. God, too, has his moves; and since he is God, he knows the game better, always sees the game as a whole, and can be counted on to win, for the good of us all. But many of humanity's moves are a real threat to his game and have to be countered. The image has its inherent limitations. It offers no neat way to build in those human beings who want God's great purposes for us all to be accomplished, but who cannot be thought of as throwing away humanity's game. What is useful in the image is the strong assertion of human freedom. God cannot coerce our moves, because he gave us freedom of choice. Therefore he is forced to outplay us. He can turn some of humanity's moves to his own purposes whereas others are sheer embarrassments. But in no case does God need to take responsibility for our moves.

The point against Grüber as Rubinstein represents him and against Rubinstein himself is that one can believe in the God of history and believe that he is *still* the God of history without having to believe that any particular event, and above all the holocaust, is God's move or God's deed. Mankind makes many moves that God need take no responsibility for. To say this is not to explain the holocaust, but it is to give oneself space and time to work on an explanation that does not require the death of the God of history.

One of the most intriguing symbolic figures in the Hebrew Bible is the Servant of the Lord (Servant of Yahweh) who appears in the poetry of the Second Isaiah (Isaiah 40–55). Christians are most familiar with the depiction of the Servant as *suffering*, in Isaiah 53. He was "a man of sorrows and acquainted with grief . . . we esteemed him stricken, smitten by God, and afflicted" (Isa. 53:3–4). Christians have this familiarity because, from earliest times, Christians have taken the suffering Servant as a prophecy of Jesus and his Passion. The crucifixion of Jesus when it first happened was evidently a stunning blow to the disciples' hopes and expectations. They were frightened, scattered, and crushed. Then came the resurrection, and their faith in Jesus was not only revived, it was lifted to new heights. God had "made him both Lord and Christ" (Acts 3:36). Now it was possible to look at the fact of Jesus' suffering and death again and to see it in a new light. Given the resurrection, the crucifixion must also have been part of God's plan. So the disciples were interested in whatever there might be in the law and prophets and psalms that could throw further light on Jesus' suffering and death. What purpose did God have in mind—what clues did the scriptures provide?

Isaiah 53 was an answer to the disciples' prayer. It spoke of the Servant of the Lord as one who seemed at first to be punished by God for his own wrongdoing, as Jesus must have seemed to the priests. But then the truth dawns on the onlookers: "He was bruised for our iniquities; . . . and with his stripes we are healed. . . . the Lord has laid on him the iniquity of us all" (Isa. 53:5–6). The Servant suffered vicariously, on behalf of others. He suffered severely, died, and was buried. But even the resurrection seems to have been predicted, for the Servant lives to see the fruit of his travail. By his suffering many are brought to salvation (Isa. 53:8–11).

It would be impossible to exaggerate the importance of Isaiah 53 to Christians, providing as it does a full-blown theology of the cross—a rationale for understanding the death of Jesus not at all as a defeat for him, but rather as the most effective of all sacrifices, guaranteeing Christians' forgiveness and their admission to the kingdom of God.

It does not at all deny the validity of seeing Jesus as an embodiment of the symbolic Servant, however, to realize that the prophet who composed the Servant poems and generations of his Jewish readers have a very different understanding of who the Servant is. To them the Servant is the people Israel—perhaps an idealized Israel, but the people Israel nevertheless. The justification for this identification is explicit in the poems themselves. The Servant is named Israel (or Jacob, the equivalent) in Isa. 44:1, 44:21, 45:4, and 49:3; "You are my servant, Israel, in whom I will be glorified."

The Servant poems make it clear that the Servant (Israel) has a task to perform for God. The task includes reconstituting national life in the Judean homeland, for the time of the poems is near the end of the Babylonian captivity (c. 540 B.C.) and a vast work of reconstruction awaits. A new exodus is about to begin, and the labors of repossessing and rebuilding the Promised Land loom. However, says the Lord, "It is too light a thing that you should be my servant to raise up the tribes of Jacob and to restore the preserved of Israel; I will give you as a light to the nations, that my salvation may reach to the end of the earth" (Isa. 49:6).

The Hebrew Bible reaches one of its universalistic peaks here. The fact that there is a chosen people does not mean to Jews that God cares nothing and has no plans for the other peoples. On the contrary, there is a chosen people for the sake of the others. The chosen people were chosen to be a light to the rest of mankind. They were chosen to receive the revelation of monotheism—"the Lord is One"—but they were also chosen to share this revelation, so that the nations would receive it, too. They were chosen to receive God's commandments; but again the Lord's eye was on the day when the commandments would have been so well advertised by obedience and ensuing justice that all nations would want to have them. "Turn to me and be saved, all the ends of the earth!" (Isa. 45:22) is another word of the Lord in this same part of Isaiah. The idea was that the ends of the earth would turn to the Lord because his people were a shining light of truth and justice. All this is testified to as Jewish belief by the Talmud.

But what of the *suffering* of the Servant? How does this fit into the picture of the Servant as the people Israel?

It is not possible to review here the history of Jewish interpretation of the suffering Servant. Nor would it be fair to suggest that everything Christians believe about Jesus in the role of the Servant can be assumed to be believed by Jews about themselves in the role of the Servant. In fact, what follows is not a Jewish suggestion at all. But it does seem possible to use some of what Christians say about the suffering Servant in an effort to assimilate the holocaust.

As we saw above, people who look on while the Servant suffers take him at first to be "smitten of God," presumably because of his own sins. But they change their minds and realize that "he was bruised for our iniquities; . . . All we like sheep have gone astray; we have turned every one to his own way; and the Lord has laid on him the iniquity of us all" (Isa. 53:5–6). Thus the onlookers are portrayed as having been brought to repentance. Jews and Christians agree pretty well about repentance. It includes confessing one's sins. The onlookers conform to that. They admit their iniquities. Repentance also includes contrition, which is acute sorrow about one's wrongdoing, acute enough to make one want never again to commit such deeds. The onlookers seem to conform to that part of the definition, too. They have been appalled at the condition of the Servant— "his appearance was so marred, . . . He was despised and rejected by men; . . . he was wounded . . . bruised . . . oppressed, . . . and cut off out of the land of the living" (Isa. 52:14–53:8). The Servant was a thoroughly pitiable figure; and admitting that, the onlookers take upon themselves the responsibility and the guilt for having brought about his condition. "He was bruised for our iniquities."

Toward the end of this poem about the suffering Servant, attention is turned to what the Servant accomplished. "He shall see the fruit of the travail of his soul and be satisfied; by his knowledge shall the righteous one, my servant, make many to be accounted righteous; and he shall bear their iniquities" (Isa. 53:11). The clearest positive achievement of the Servant is that he makes many righteous. "The many" who are made righteous are definitely identified with those whose iniquities he has borne, which means that the many are such as the onlookers we have been considering whose iniquities the Servant has borne. The only fact about the onlookers that would account for their being made righteous is that they have been brought by the Servant's sufferings to repentance. This is evidently also the meaning of the lines, "Upon him was the chastisement that *made us whole*, and with his stripes *we are healed*" (Isa. 53:5; italics mine). The onlookers are whole and healed then with reference to their repentance, which leads directly to their forgiveness and recovery of righteousness in their relations with the Servant.

Can this notion of how the suffering Servant brings many to righteousness be related to the holocaust? It can be if the sight of the six million so marred in appearance, so bruised and oppressed, and cut off from the land of the living, will move the onlookers to repentance. For that to happen, the onlookers would have to see that the six million were "wounded for our transgressions and bruised for our iniquities." And they would have to come to hate with all their hearts the transgressions and iniquities within them that caused the wounding and the killing.

This would mean that *Christian* onlookers of the holocaust would be brought to repentance and made righteous.

"Repentance for what?"

For the antisemitism in us.

"Why in *us*? We had nothing to do with causing the holocaust."

That is so—nothing to do with the holocaust legally, factually, in ordinary history. But it was antisemitism like ours that conceived of the holocaust, tolerated it, cooperated with it, made it happen.

"What do you mean, 'antisemitism like ours'?—we Christians are not antisemitic."

Really? Will you give me the time to give you the evidence?

The argument is a bit complicated. Let us consider it step by step.

1. There is much antisemitism among Christians.

2. There is secularized antisemitism, such as characterized the Nazis, which derives from Christian antisemitism.

3. The holocaust was caused by antisemitism.

4. The holocaust is the revelation of the full horror of the sin of antisemitism.

5. A revelation of the horrifying consequences of one's acknowledged sin can lead to repentance and to being healed of the sin.

Each of these assertions needs some amplification and documentation.

1. There is much antisemitism among Christians. Like any other trait that occurs in Christians, it varies from person to person. No doubt there are Christians who are completely free of it. On the other hand, there are sources of antisemitism built into Christian tradition and Christian history, and all Christians are therefore exposed to it.

To assert that Christians are, as a community, marked by antisemitism is to be offensive, of course. No one likes to be called a dirty name, and "antisemite" is a dirty name in our society. The consequence is that even the most belligerent antisemites do not refer to themselves as antisemites. They are "anti-Zionists," with the implication that their objection is to Zionist "imperialism." Or they believe in freedom of religion, but what they are fighting against is "Jewish character" or Jewish "control of public life." No one calls himself a bigot.

Even so, in spite of the disguises and rationales that extreme anti-Jewish bigotry assumes, most Christians identify it as extreme, and do not want to be part of it. Therefore if only extreme antisemitism counted as antisemitism, most Christians could fairly claim not to be involved. But antisemitism is a matter of degrees.

Antisemitism is usually defined as hostility toward Jews simply because they are Jews. That is, antisemitism is an instance of prejudice and operates with stereotypes. Among the prejudiced, one does not have to have evidence that a particular individual with green skin hates motherhood. The stereotype over-assures one that it is the nature of green-skins to hate motherhood. As in the case of other stereotypes that are encountered in dealing with prejudice, the stereotype of the Jew already includes the vices one detests. So one needs no more information to justify one's hostility against Jews than that the objects of the hostility are Jewish. Just so, some of us grew up in communities in which the stereotype of the Jew so effectively enveloped the actual Jew that one never got to know him and never had a chance to detect his virtues and his charities; one knew from the stereotype that he was a "Christ-killer," or a condemned soul, excluded from God's forgiveness. Since all Christians have been exposed to contamination by this prejudice, how can any Christian be sure that he has not been infected by it? How can he be sure that a "mild case" is not fraught with possibly fatal danger for someone?

We noticed on some earlier pages the estrangement of Jews and Christians that developed in the earliest days of Christianity, following the resurrection. Christians saw the life, death, and resurrection of Jesus as the climax of sacred history—Jews did not see it as sacred history at all. Judaism and Christianity were making mutually exclusive assertions: Jesus is the Messiah —or he is not. The commandments of Moses are authoritative for all time to come—or, Christ is the end of the law for them that believe. Jews are the true people of God—or, Christians are the true Israel. The old covenant is valid forever—or, the "new covenant" has invalidated the old. Thus far we have only religious controversy.

But we also saw that when the Roman empire became "Christian," Christianity gained the use of the power of the state as a weapon against the Jews. Jews were forbidden to proselytize and were put under increasingly severe disabilities. They were excluded from careers in politics and in the military services and from more and more civilian livelihoods. *This was antisemitic behavior by a Christian society and state.* Meanwhile various of the church fathers both urged the government on and inflamed the populace with all sorts of charges of immorality against the Jews and above all with the charge of deicide: killing Christ. Synagogues were burned, Jews were endangered and killed. Over and over again it came to seem intolerable to various Christian monks, bishops, and eventually even reformers that Judaism persisted when by their reckoning it should have disappeared into Christianity with the coming of the Messiah. If the Jews themselves did not believe the Messiah had come, how were the Christian laity to be sure that he had come—particularly if they were constantly exposed to Jews? So Jews were driven away, kept out of sight in ghettos, and slaughtered all through Western history. *All this is antisemitic behavior by Christians.*

Nothing sufficiently momentous has yet happened to purge anti-Jewish propaganda and anti-Jewish sentiment from Christian tradition, and they are still present in today's American Christian mentality. This is the conclusion reached in a study referred to earlier, *Christian Beliefs and Anti-Semitism*, by Charles Glock and Rodney Stark.*

Glock and Stark based their conclusions on an elaborate questionnaire study of Christians in California, which they subsequently confirmed by a national survey. They discovered that where certain widespread Christian styles of believing flow together and reinforce each other, there is found a high incidence of negative opinions about Jews. One of these styles of believing is very literal-minded. Biblical statements and statements of church teaching are taken as absolutist formulas, without the feeling for nuances that is fostered by an understanding of literary styles, symbolic uses of language, historical conditions, and changes in human perspectives and values. Another of these styles of believing is "particularism," a term applied to those adherents of any system of beliefs who believe that theirs is the only true system and that other systems, wherever they disagree, must be in error. The true system of belief, particular-

*Charles Glock and Rodney Stark, *Christian Beliefs and Anti-Semitism* (New York: Harper & Row, 1966).

ists hold, is open to anyone who wishes to adhere to it. But anyone who passes it by is doomed to be excluded by God from the rewards that he is holding in store for true believers. Glock and Stark found that generally the more literal-minded a person was, the more particularist he was likely to be, and that literalist and particularist Christians were loaded with derogatory judgments about Jews. For them, for example, Abraham, David, Solomon, and other such figures from the Hebrew Bible whom Christians rate highly are taken to be Christians before Christ. They are not identified as Jews at all, but as Christians! Whereas the other disciples of Jesus are seen as Christians, such a figure as Judas, of course, is clearly identified as a Jew.

Christians who exhibited anti-Jewish opinions and feelings were distributed unevenly among the various denominations. Nevertheless, as late as 1966 in this era of ecumenism according to Glock and Stark (their findings bear repetition): More than half of American Protestants affirmed as at least possibly true (some were sure it was true) the proposition that "the Jews can never be forgiven for what they did to Jesus until they accept Him as the True Savior" (p. 61). More than a third of American Protestants affirmed as at least possibly true the proposition, "The reason the Jews have so much trouble is because God is punishing them for rejecting Jesus" (p. 63).

The viciousness of such beliefs lies precisely in their potential as ideology, that is, as rationalizations for hostile behavior toward Jews. If God himself has not forgiven the Jews and is still engaged in punishing them, what a grand excuse I have for punishing them myself, when I have a chance, and for condoning the actions of others who make trouble for Jews.

So, as we have seen, there is a large amount of erroneous derogatory opinion about Jews current among Christians, and it feeds into and gets expressed as unsympathetic and hostile behavior of Christians toward Jews. Where does derogatory opinion about Jews among Christians come from? It is heavy with items from New Testament history. Therefore it must come from Christian sources. It derives from misunderstood or correctly understood but erroneous teaching by Christians.

2. There is also a *secularized* antisemitism, such as characterized Hitler and the Nazis. It is secular in the sense that it employs no Christian premises for its opinions—it makes no appeal to Christian history or theology. It is secularized in the sense that it is derivative from centuries of Christian antisemitism. What had once been at root a specifically Christian hostility in Europe had in some quarters acquired all sorts of nonreligious rationalizations. The Middle Ages produced stories of Jewish ritual murder of Christians, of Jewish need for Christian blood for Passover, of Jews poisoning Christians' wells, of the Jewish dissemination of the Black Death. One can only explain the stories as products of the animosity that Christian teaching had inspired. No doubt the stories themselves produced new hostility. But they are stories that have no basis in either Jewish or Christian religious beliefs or practices. They are as ignorant of religion as they are nonreligious.

In modern times there has been a similar development of nonreligious rationalizations for hatred of Jews. One of these has centered in bogus notions of race. On the one hand, the Nazis worked hard at popularizing the notion that the German people were prime examples of the superior "Aryan race." On the other hand they identified the Jews as an alien and inferior "race." On these grounds it could be argued that to tolerate the presence of Jews in Germany was to encourage the mixing of unequal heredities and the hybridization and weakening of the "master race." It has, of course, been repeatedly shown that talking about race in terms such as these is nonsense. There is not and never was an "Aryan race" (there is only a family of Aryan languages); and neither the Germans nor the Jews are examples of a race, let alone the idea of a "pure" race. There has been so much human mobility and intermarriage that there is only one race of human beings, that is, the human race.

Another rationalization of Nazi hostility to the Jews centered on the story that Jews were engaged in a world-wide conspiracy to control the world. Whatever was taken ill in any quarter, labor unions and strikes or monopolies and shortages of goods and high prices, revolutions or reactionary movements, all could be referred to the "Jewish conspiracy." If there was no shred of evidence connecting any of these items with Jews, that just went to show how clever the conspirators were in covering their tracks.

In reality, however, Jews in early twentieth-century Europe were as diverse in their economic positions and political points of view as the populations of which they were a part. The clearest proof of that is that they did not even possess enough organization to be able to warn each other of Hitler's intentions for them. Millions of Jews might have saved themselves if most of them had not been taken so much by surprise.

So there was a secularized antisemitism rampant in Nazi Germany. Why does one assert that it was derived from Christian antisemitism? Part of the answer has been given above. In the Middle Ages already, when there was no other framework of thought to draw on but the Christian tradition, Christian hostility to Jews still created nonreligious rationalizations for itself out of sheer evil imaginings, such as we saw in the rumors about Jewish complicity in the Black Death. If Jews in their wretched, overcrowded ghettos locally fell victims to the Black Death, they were branded as the source of it. If the Jews with their high standards of cleanliness largely escaped the Black Death locally, it was claimed that they knew how to produce it for Christians and to escape it themselves.

There is further evidence in the Glock and Stark study that connects Christian antisemitic beliefs with secular antisemitism.

Current specifically "Christian" (that is, religion-based) anti-semitic beliefs correlate highly among Americans with such secular antisemitic beliefs as that a Jew is more likely than a Christian to cheat in his business dealings, tends to be exceptionally self-centered, touchy, and socially exclusive, is probably soft on communism, and is more loyal to Israel than to the United States. Thus the adverse opinions regarding Jews held by Christians on religious grounds ("God is punishing them for what they did to Jesus") either prompt or reinforce their secular antisemitic beliefs ("Jews are avaricious"). The study also indicated that Christians who hold negative *beliefs* about Jews as persons tend very strongly to admit to *feeling* unfriendly or hostile toward Jews. And finally, Christians who hold negative beliefs about Jews and have unfriendly feelings toward Jews indicated readiness to behave in ways that discriminate against Jews. For example, such Christians supported the exclusion of Jews from resort hotels and were unmotivated to challenge a verbal attack on a Jewish storekeeper who had been called "a crook like all the Jews." In short, the evidence is that specifically religious beliefs about Jews, as that they have been "rejected by God" because of their past or present relationship to Jesus, foster a whole range of antisemitic beliefs, feelings, and actions with reference to Jews that are not ostensibly connected with Christian or Jewish religion.

3. The holocaust was caused by antisemitism. The slaughter of six million Jews by the Nazis was a *pure* case, as well as the most heart-rending and ultimate expression, of antisemitism, for antisemitism is hatred of Jews solely because they are Jews. Jews were not arrested and then tried for alleged crimes. There was but one crime: being Jewish, and it was a crime punishable by death. Jews were rounded up by trainsful and shipped to extermination camps. As indicated earlier, they were classified as they entered the camps. The little children, the feeble, and the ill were consigned to immediate death; the able-bodied were

spared to be worked to death, that is, to work under dehumanizing conditions and brutal discipline until they, too, were feeble or ill, when they would be selected for the gas chambers. The "final solution" for the Nazis of "the Jewish question" was the death of all Jews.

The Nazis themselves were chiefly secularist antisemites. Hitler hated Christianity as he hated Judaism, so much so that it has been suggested by several Jewish writers that he was venting his combined anti-Christian and anti-Jewish fury on the Jews alone because they were defenseless and a safe target.

But what of the German people generally? There was opposition to Nazi measures against the Jews, there were efforts to sabotage the extermination machinery here and there, there were Christians who risked much to create "underground railways" for Jewish escape. But by and large there must have been great reservoirs of antisemitism in Europe that Hitler knew he could count on for creating and staffing the extermination machinery, for tolerating the slaughter without protest, for knowing about the horror and yet carrying on without loss of morale or patriotism. Whether it was explicitly Christian antisemitism or derived, secularized antisemitism—and even Hitler was quoted as saying that in "defending [himself] against the Jew" he was fighting for "the Lord"*—it was antisemitism that conceived, organized, carried out, and rationalized the holocaust.

Furthermore, it was *all degrees* of antisemitism working together that made the holocaust possible. There had to be fanatic types of antisemites who were capable of conceiving the final solution and visualizing the gruesome details and giving the orders. But equally necessary to the holocaust were the masses of antisemites of low degree who only had to be antisemitic enough to think that, although they themselves would have had no direct part in it, the Jews must deserve it, or that it was

*Glock and Stark, *Christian Beliefs and Anti-Semitism*, p. xv.

none of the citizen's business to inquire into it, or that it was too dangerous to do anything to help Jews to escape or otherwise to interfere, or that it really could not be true.

4. The holocaust is the revelation of the full horror of the sin of antisemitism. Any slight injustice to a human being is a cause of concern and anger if we take that human being seriously, if we are close to him. Any slight injury to a Jew for no other reason than that he is a Jew is such an injustice and properly excites concern and anger. With what words then shall we attempt to respond to the mental anguish, physical pain, indignity, and death inflicted on six million human beings for no other reason than that they were Jews? And if the holocaust is the direct consequence of antisemitism, what language is strong enough for the condemnation of antisemitism? And if any degree of antisemitism, however low, played its part in producing the holocaust, at what level is antisemitism to be safely ignored, tolerated, or excused? What is a safe amount of the causation of history's biggest and worst crime? How much of the ingredients of the holocaust are Christians going to expect God indulgently to overlook in themselves? "Everyone who is angry with his brother shall be liable to judgment" (Matt. 5:22).

5. A revelation of the horrifying consequences of one's acknowledged sin can lead to repentance and to being healed of the sin. However much the terms "Christian" and "antisemitic," as Jules Isaac remarked, "jar on one another," and however much it ought to be the case that they mutually contradict and exclude each other, the fact is that the Christian community is tainted by varying amounts of antisemitism. To be open to the evidence and to accept the fact is to acknowledge that antisemitism is among our sins as Christians. How incomparably dangerous the sin of antisemitism is has been revealed in its causing of the holocaust. Christians have therefore been brought to the brink of repentance. It becomes possible for the holocaust to

have the kind of effect on us that the cross of Christ does. We can say of the victims that they bore our sins in their own bodies in the death camps. "We esteemed [them] stricken, smitten of God, and afflicted. But [they were] wounded for our transgressions; . . . All we like sheep have gone astray; . . . and the Lord has laid on [them] the iniquity of us all" (Isa. 53:4–6).

The crucifixion of Jesus ought to have redeemed Christians from one sin above all, and that is complicity in—or even toleration of—arbitrary and inhuman attacks on the innocent. For what sin did Jesus more obviously bear in his body than this one? He suffered innocently in that he suffered without any due process that established his guilt for a punishable offense. He also suffered indignities and physical pains that no human society ought to accept as appropriate punishment for any crime. In the holocaust, too, there was no due process that proved any Jew's guilt of anything. There was suffering that no crimes could have merited. The holocaust proves, therefore, that not all Christians have yet been redeemed from this sin of inhuman attack on the innocent. Is it too much to hope that the combination of the crucifixion and the holocaust will at last produce the repentance by which God will heal us of this sin?

To see the holocaust in these terms is to weep the tears of shame and guilt. It is to be shocked and embarrassed before God. It is to hate the sin in us that has proved so malignant, to give it up, and to want and pray never to fall into it again. It is to be ready to suffer whatever judgment the Lord God finds it necessary to pronounce upon us. It is to want to make restitution to the survivors for the terrors visited upon the victims. In short, it is to repent.

Repentance is painful and is never easy. But it is the one condition for being forgiven. It is also the beginning of God's process of healing us of the sin of which we repent. Sin in us is a stubborn condition. The process of sanctification is long and calls in both the Christian and Jewish traditions for the practice of daily repentance. But the hope is placed before us that the holocaust and Christian repentance for antisemitism can bring the end of Christian antisemitism.

Does it need to be added that to think of the holocaust in the way just indicated is not to reconcile oneself to it, not to justify it, not at all to try to see it as an act of God intended to bring good in its wake? One wants to agree with Emil Fackenheim that no religious *meaning* is ever to be found in Auschwitz, and that to seek one is blasphemy; what one wants to find is the religious *response* that is called for. Fackenheim goes on to say that the Jews who died in the holocaust were not martyrs. That is, they did not volunteer for death, and they did not die for their faith. They died because they had been identified by some others as Jews. Yet, there is a sense in which they were martyrs. They were unwilling witnesses to us of the awful vulnerability of Jews in the face of demonic antisemitism. As such they are a Sinai-like imperative to us Christians to exorcise the demons of antisemitism from ourselves and from the world.

5

COVENANT

More than half of all American Protestants hold as at least possibly true the proposition that "the Jews can never be forgiven for what they did to Jesus until they accept Him as the True Savior," according to the Glock and Stark study mentioned earlier. We identified Christians who tended to agree with this proposition as "particularist," because what they mean to say is that the only way for Jews to be saved is through faith in Jesus as savior. Particularists believe that there is only one way to be saved—their way.

Now there are two questions that ought to be raised about the particularist Christian position as it bears upon Jews. One is what effect it has on Christian attitudes toward Jews and on Jewish feelings—this is a moral question. The other is whether it is really necessary for Christians to be particularist, or whether particularism is an accident that has nothing essential to do with being Christian—this is a theological question.

What effect does particularism in Christians have on Christian attitudes toward Jews and on Jewish sensibilities? We have already seen that it can be a ground for religious hostility toward Jews in that a disproportionately large percentage of particularist Christians, compared with other Christians, *are* hostile to Jews. We have also seen that persons who are hostile toward Jews on religious grounds are prone to believe the worst about Jews in matters that have nothing to do with religion and thus to participate in secular antisemitism as well. This ought to be disturbing to all Christians.

There is another aspect to this question. Particularist Christians have strong inclinations toward proselytizing. If there is only one way to be saved and that is to believe as they do, and if they are commanded to love all mankind and therefore to want to see all mankind saved, they are obliged to want to convert all mankind to believing as they do. Thus particularist Christians are much more heavily involved in conversionist missionary operations among the "unsaved" than are Christians generally, and for them the unsaved include the Jews.

When the conversionist effort fails, there is danger of resentment among the missionaries. The story of Martin Luther's relations with the Jews is illustrative. As pointed out earlier, Luther, in his early days as a reformer, deplored the abuses that had been heaped on Jews during the Middle Ages. He thought it was scandalous that Christians had given Jews good reasons to hate the name of Christ, in whose name they had been tormented. If that were to go on, how could Jews ever come to the truth in Christ? So Luther counseled Christian love toward Jews. He had high hopes that once Christian behavior toward Jews established Christian credibility among Jews, the pure light of the rediscovered gospel would win them over to becoming Christians. However, as much as Luther's preaching may have led to better treatment of Jews, Jews did not respond to the gospel. They continued to believe that they were already in covenant with the one true God. Luther resented the rebuff to the gospel. From being the loudest Christian voice calling for love toward the kinsmen of Jesus, he became, we have seen, their angry enemy, calling for the burning of synagogues and the expulsion of Jews from the kingdoms of Europe.

Christians may also be interested in contemplating the effect on Jews of being subjected to strenuous efforts to convert them. Many Christians have experienced what it is like to be badgered by some of the more aggressive of Jehovah's Witnesses. Up to a point I may find it moving to taste the concern of a stranger for my salvation. But if the conversation goes on to reveal his total rejection of my faith and hope of salvation, and if I am faced with the demand to give up my faith in favor of his, the outcome is likely to be alienation between us. He may have great assurance and joy in his convictions. But how could he possibly know that my convictions are groundless and useless for relating me to the Redeemer God?

Very often in a conversation that has been initiated with a view to proselytizing one of us, what offends us is the proselytizer's ignorance of what we know, and of the good ground we stand on in knowing what we know. We are not merely defensive; we are not merely determined to give a good account of ourselves as debaters, as though the matters at issue were wholly academic. We are likely to have thought a good deal about our spiritual heritage and to have heard many questions raised about its validity. We have worked our way through these questions. We may feel with the author of 2 Timothy, "But I am not ashamed, for I know whom I have believed, and I am sure that he is able to guard until that Day what has been entrusted to me" (2 Tim. 1:12). In the light of that, it is not persuasive to listen to the arguments of a person who does not understand our position as well as we do. Who is he to tell us ours is a false position when we understand our position and he does not? Who is he to demand that we accept his position when we do not understand it? And what if it further crosses our minds that he does not understand his own position as well as we understand ours and is appealing not to understanding, but to dogmatic formulas and to rote learning?

We can better understand the Jewish target of particularist

Christian proselytizing when we put ourselves in a comparable place. The Jew is not to be expected to be an easy mark for proselytizing. He does not experience his religion as bankrupt or inferior. He understands the splendor of his tradition and the reasons for prizing it. He too knows whom he has believed. He is fully as confident of standing in a covenant relationship with God as Christians are. Why should he change, particularly on the suggestion of someone who does not understand what the Jew already has? Furthermore, even if he felt that he could be equally at home spiritually in another faith-community, it is likely to seem repugnant to him even to imagine abandoning his people in what he sees as their depleted and precarious condition.

Jews have another reaction to proselytizers, learned from centuries-long contact with those who have simply wished them out of existence *as Jews*, saying, "Be baptized or begone." The Marranos of Spain and Portugal accepted baptism as preferable to death in the fourteenth and fifteenth centuries. But having made a gesture of outward conformity to the demand for conversion, they continued to practice Judaism and to raise their children more or less secretly as Jews in the privacy of their homes. Then they were subjected to the Inquisition as heretical Christians and many were tortured and killed. In the days of Heinrich Heine in nineteenth-century Germany, Jews were told, "Be baptized or be left out of the world of those who have their music played and their books published." Proselytization has seemed to Jews over the years to express above all else the rejection of them as Jews. It is possible for Jews to raise the question, as they have, whether it is worth preserving one's own Judaism at the cost of the disabilities and dangers one thereby bequeaths to children and grandchildren. But Jews for the most part have had too much pride to give up Judaism for security, and they have simply not been convinced that there is any better religion for which to give it up. Hence they are likely for the most part to take any effort to convert them as itself a hostile act. It does not seem so much the act of a benefactor as the act of one who does not grant Jews the right to exist as Jews.

Christian particularism has sometimes led to hostile feelings toward Jews and at other times to efforts to convert Jews to Christianity. For their part, Jews have often felt that the one consequence was as threatening to them as the other.

Therefore, how Christian is Christian particularism? Is it really of the essence of Christianity to be particularist, especially in its relations with Jews?

An answer is suggested by the experiences Christians have had during recent years in the ecumenical movement. Before ecumenism, relations between Protestant denominations were strained at best; relations between Protestant and Catholic churches did not exist. In short, we were all more or less particularist, no Christian being easy in his mind that persons in churches other than his own were safe. But the ecumenical movement built upon, and then strengthened, the conviction that the churches, underneath their verbal differences, held very fundamental commitments in common. As efforts were made to resolve the verbal differences, it became increasingly clear to many that each church's verbal formulas were less than ultimate. Human beings, even the composers of church confessions, are men and not God. In their human limitedness, they fall short of understanding the mysteries of God. In their human sinfulness, they are misled by partisanship, pride, and stubbornness. All their theological products, even those confessions of faith with the greatest prestige in the respective churches, turn out to be historically conditioned approximations of the truths the churches want to proclaim. As a consequence of this new relativism and especially of the sense of a God-given mandate to pursue Christian unity, the churches have surprised the world with their new agreements, limited as they are, about the ministry, the Eucharist, the Papacy, and other matters.

Christians have discovered that elements of teaching and practice that are central in their own traditions, and that they take to be of the essence of true religion and necessary to salvation, are present in the traditions of other churches. Perhaps these elements are not instantly visible. Frequently they require learning a new vocabulary in order to recognize them. But they are there and, finding them, we can rejoice. We rejoice because we like to find allies in a matter of primary importance to us. Both we and the truth as we see it have gained reinforcements.

Christians have also discovered that the heritages of churches other than their own include items that are absent from or underemphasized in their own traditions but that appeal to them as valuable. When the churches went their separate ways, each could take pride only in what it possessed. But with the pooling of heritages through study and dialogue, each church is enriched by all the others. All the churches gain in that all may borrow from each other freely without subtracting anything from each other. At the same time all the churches tend to become more unified in that all tend to become more catholic, that is, more representative of what all the churches have always and everywhere been.

Christians have discovered in their ecumenical experiences that the need to proselytize each other and the guilt-feeling for not proselytizing fall away. In short, a certain kind of particularism—Christian particularism with reference to other sects of Christianity—tends to disappear. If the denominations discover that they have more in common than they thought, and that they are in the process of becoming more inclusive and more alike all the time, then conversion of adherents from one denomination to another becomes at once easier and of less interest.

In the present ecumenical situation it is natural that the proselytizing model of what it means to do "missionary work" or "evangelism" gives way to a "witnessing" model. Proselytizing means getting someone to give up one religious belief system and affiliation and to take on another. The process makes sense when one who has the truth confronts one who has been brought up in error. Witnessing, on the other hand, means describing one's own beliefs and the experiences on which they rest. Its spirit is not belligerent or triumphal. It wants to share the good news it has. It offers rather than imposes something. Witnessing also implies being open to having others testify to matters of which they have knowledge. Witnessing makes sense when the situation is such that no participant possesses all the truth and no participant is without truth. And it is this situation which ecumenically minded Christians have agreed is the actual condition in which the churches find themselves today.

What will happen if Christians carry over the same ecumenical spirit and witnessing approach to their relations with Jews?

At the outset there would have to be only an assumption among Christians that Jews and Christians have something in common religiously. But what could be more evident than that they do? Christianity began as a movement within Judaism. Its founder, all its original adherents, and all the apostles who carried on the movement after Jesus were Jews. More than that, Christianity's origins were exclusively Jewish. Sometimes in the history of religions one encounters a new development that was inspired by the encounter of two previously independent religious traditions. Thus Nanak in the sixteenth century founded Sikhism as a blend of Hinduism and Islam. But there is no evidence of any non-Jewish influence upon Jesus. The Bible of the Jews was the scripture out of which Christianity was first preached; and even after the whole New Testament had been published, the Bible of the Jews continued to be Christian scripture.

Given the origin of Christianity in Judaism and the continuance of Jewish themes in the development of Christianity, it seems promising to approach Judaism in an ecumenical spirit rather than from a particularist stance. Can Christians discover in Judaism elements of teaching and practice that are central also in Christianity, that seem essential to true religion and necessary for salvation? And if so, where should one look?

It is commonly said that Judaism is a religion of deeds rather than of beliefs. It is sometimes even claimed that Judaism has no theology at all, and that orthodoxy (correct teaching) in Judaism really refers to orthopraxis (correct practice). It is true that Jewish emphasis is placed on doing, more than on believing, and that there is no Jewish *dogma* in the sense of a creed or formula of belief that is binding on Jews. But in the course of their development of the classical Jewish tradition, the rabbis who created the authoritative Talmud and Midrash produced an extensive theology. Midrash is exegesis and exposition of biblical books, notably the Pentateuch. The Talmud is the written version of what once was the oral law and of the further development of it. In both bodies of material the ancient rabbis were on the one hand interpreting and applying the biblical law and the spirit of that law, and on the other hand preaching and telling stories with a view to explaining and justifying the ways of God to man. That is, they were doing theology.

Ever since the beginning of the modernist developments that took hold in Judaism in the nineteenth century, there has been no uniformity of Jewish practice, much less of Jewish belief. Nevertheless, the doctrine of the Talmud and Midrash remains immensely influential through the teaching of the rabbis today, and provides the norm by which all variations of Jewish religious belief are measured. A convenient way for Christians to become acquainted with Talmudic and Midrashic theology is to read *Aspects of Rabbinic Theology* by Solomon Schechter.*

We have already looked at Jewish beliefs about the Messiah. Here we found a clear divergence between Jewish and Christian thought, in that Talmudic as well as prophetic ideas were

---

*Solomon Schechter, *Aspects of Rabbinic Theology* (New York: Schocken Books, 1961).

focused on a this-worldly age of the Messiah whereas Christian thought has tended to spiritualize the Messiahship as the reign of Christ the king in his church and in the hearts of men. Even this statement must be qualified by calling attention to the millennialist tradition in Christianity, according to which Christ is expected to reign for a thousand years over a peaceful world before dwelling with the saints in heaven (Revelation 20). In any case, Christianity shares with Judaism the underlying conviction basic to all Messianic thought and central to both faiths, namely, that God is the Lord of history and will someday bring mankind into a state of joyful obedience to his will.

Since Jesus taught Jews about God with frequent references to the Hebrew Bible, there is no question but that Christians (as followers of Jesus) and Jews worship and speak about the same God. One sometimes hears in Christian circles about the "God of wrath" portrayed in the Old Testament and the "God of love" revealed in the New Testament. This suggests some confusion among Christians which may even include in some cases the notion that two different Gods are being spoken of. But the confusion is unnecessary, because it rests on insufficient acquaintance with the Bible. The one and only God of both testaments is actually seen as a God of wrath *and* as a God of love in both testaments. The "wrath" of God refers to God's capacity for judgment upon wickedness. We see the wrath referred to in the Hebrew Bible, to be sure. But it is also pointed to repeatedly in the New Testament, for example, in the Sermon on the Mount: "Every tree that does not bear good fruit is cut down and thrown into the fire" (Matt. 7:19). The "love of God" points to his providential care and his merciful readiness to forgive and to save. The theme is as evident in the Hebrew Bible as it is in the New Testament, as the psalms abundantly disclose: for example, "O continue thy steadfast love to those who know thee, and thy salvation to the upright of heart!" (Ps. 36:10).

Jewish and Christian thought about God come very close to one another again in seeing the work of God in this world as threefold: God is Creator of all things; God is Revealer of himself and of his will for mankind; and God is Redeemer, who lifts up the fallen and who forgives and restores. The biblical *creation* story is one and the same for Jews and Christians. The chief paradigm of *revelation* for Jews is the event at Mount Sinai, when God gave Moses the law by which his people were to know how to do his will. The model-event of *redemption* for Jews is God's action in freeing his people from Egypt under the leadership of Moses. For Christians, Jesus himself, thought of as the incarnate Word of God, is the key to God's revelation of himself. And the death and resurrection of Jesus are for Christians the supreme symbol of God's work of redemption.

Nevertheless, for all the differences of the symbols, there is here a vast area of agreement in matters of the highest religious importance. For both Jews and Christians God is serious about human righteousness. Whether through the written and oral Torah or through the Lordship of Jesus as the Christ, God is seen as determined to bring mankind to the peace and freedom inherent in learning to obey his holy will. For both Jews and Christians, the work of revelation is not locked up in the past; it goes on steadily wherever there is (as Jews say) study of Torah or (as Christians say) a looking to Jesus. Jews and Christians also have a large area of agreement with reference to redemption. For both, God responds graciously in view of the great gulf that exists between righteousness, as God both commands and hopes for it, and our actual behavior. In both religious traditions God is understood as making provisions for confession of sins, repentance, and restitution on our part and as offering full forgiveness and reconciliation with himself.

We can hardly survey Jewish theology in the space at our disposal. What we have seen is just a few of the instances in which Judaism and Christianity use the same or similar language to talk about similar beliefs of the utmost importance to both. It also suggests that if we were to go on through the doctrine of man, of sin, of salvation, we would continue to find common elements. The promise for ecumenical-style witnessing but not proselytizing dialogue between Jews and Christians must then appear excellent. The promise is that both parties will feel reinforced by each other and enriched by each others' perceptions of the common treasure: elements not only held in common but seen on both sides as of the essence of true religion. It is the promise, further, that Christians will discover biblical elements that are absent or underemphasized in their traditions but are vigorously present in Judaism, where their value and attractiveness are made evident. Perhaps Jews will find such elements in Christianity. In both cases, they will not be copyrighted, but freely available for imitation or adoption.

The ultimate outcome of such dialogue is certain to be the loss of the Christian need to proselytize Jews. Christians will more and more agree that Jews have in their own tradition all the resources that God needs to save them. Christians will know that a Jew can be saved as a Jew. At this point they can stand at the extreme antithesis of antisemitism, that is, at the place where with all their hearts they affirm the being of every Jew as a Jew.

It remains difficult for some Christians to accept this position in the face of the particularism that is asserted in the New Testament itself: "I am the way, the truth, and the life; no one comes to the Father but by me" (John 14:6).

One thing that we may note about this passage is that it is found in the Gospel of John. This Gospel is in a class by itself, compared with the Synoptic Gospels: Matthew, Mark, and Luke. The latter are seen by New Testament scholars as largely the writing down of items of oral tradition about Jesus that were circulated by the preaching of the apostles. They are believed therefore to preserve actual sayings of Jesus and to give us the typical style of Jesus' teaching. When we have studied that teaching as recorded in the Synoptics and then move to a study of the teaching of Jesus in John's Gospel, we are bound to notice a great difference both in the content and in the style. In the Synoptics, Jesus talks typically about God, the kingdom of God, and the moral expectations God has of those who hope to live in his kingdom. The style of Jesus in the Synoptics is characterized by the use of parables and striking figurative language. In the fourth Gospel, in contrast, Jesus is pictured as speaking in a very different style and largely about himself. The two ways of speaking are so different that it is easy to conclude that Jesus must have spoken in one manner or the other, but could hardly have spoken in both. If the Synoptic Gospels are full of actual reminiscences of Jesus' teaching, then the Gospel of John is not. A widely accepted theory of John's Gospel is that it is to a large extent a statement of beliefs about Jesus and his mission put in the literary form of a Gospel narrative. That is, the speeches attributed to Jesus are often statements of the evangelist's beliefs about Jesus that have, as a literary device, been presented as statements by Jesus himself. If this is so, then John 14:6 can be read as follows: John (the evangelist himself) said, "Jesus is the way, the truth, and the life; no one comes to the Father but by him."

We have before us then a very enthusiastic recommendation of Jesus. It has the effect of saying, "Jesus has proved to be my savior, he has truly showed me the way of salvation and through him I have found the Father; no one else could have saved me as he has; in fact, no one else can save anyone the way Jesus can."

So far as this paraphrase is a positive statement about Jesus' worth to John, it commands our respect. He is reporting his own experience and his feelings about it. But as we often say with reference to enthusiasts, he is right in what he affirms, wrong in what he denies. When he talks about what no one else could have done for him and what no one else can do for anyone, he is not talking about his own experience. He is talking about something that in the nature of reality he cannot possibly know about. Therefore he is not conveying facts; what he is conveying is the powerful positive *feeling* he has about what Jesus has done for him.

Perhaps all particularist statements, in and out of the New Testament, can be taken in this way: not as if they were offered as statements of fact, to the effect that there is only one true faith, but as expressions of feeling by those who are thrilled about what their faith has done for them.

We noted above that there are particularist statements in the New Testament. If we consider the canonical authority of the New Testament and the tremendous role it plays in the liturgy of the churches and in the informing of Christian preaching and education, it is no wonder that Christian particularism has been constantly reinforced. But the New Testament is far from being totally particularist and it is only fair to set particularist New Testament statements in the light of those that do justice to the Jews as people of God.

It is useful to look at the Apostle Paul's notion that what God has done through Christ is to add gentiles to the people of God by grafting wild olive branches onto the trunk of the olive tree which is Israel. The figure speaks for itself. The old olive tree has not been cut down and cast into the fire. It remains alive and fruitful. But in order that gentiles, too, may be made fruitful unto God, God has grafted them onto Israel. The life that flows into Christian gentiles is the life of Israel, typified by Abraham, the paradigm of faith. Christians are spiritual descendants of Abraham.

The vignettes of Jesus in the Synoptic Gospels are not particularist. The denunciations by Jesus of his fellow-countrymen are properly viewed as Jewish religious self-criticism. Jesus is not rejecting their faith in God, but the poor way in which they are living up to their faith, as present-day ministers and rabbis chide their own congregations. Implicit in all these scenes is Jesus' conviction that the resources of God that are available to his people are sufficient for their salvation.

Consider the parable of the rich man in the Gospel according to Luke (16: 19–31). There was a poor man named Lazarus, full of sores, who was laid at the rich man's gate, and who hoped for some of the crumbs that fell from the rich man's table. The rich man never invited Lazarus in, or sent a meal out to him, or had a physician look at his sores. He died and went to a place of torment. Lazarus also died and went to "Abraham's bosom." The expression is interesting. Clearly it refers to paradise, and who is in charge there but Abraham? Abraham is not just there, in paradise; he plays a role much like that assigned to Peter in Christian stories, standing at the gate and deciding who does and does not get in. Later on, the rich man wants Abraham to send Lazarus to his brothers, to warn them lest they also come where he is, in torment. "Abraham said, 'They have Moses and the prophets; let them hear them.' And he said, 'No, father Abraham; but if some one goes to them from the dead, they will repent.' He said to him, 'If they do not hear Moses and the prophets, neither will they be convinced if some one should rise from the dead' " (Luke 16:29–31).

What appears to be the primary teaching point of the parable is the warning given to the rich, who may fall into heartlessness and neglect their desperately poor brothers. That is to say, the parable is not directed to the nature of the after-life, or even to the question how one qualifies for paradise. Nevertheless, it asserts very strongly that whoever has Moses and the prophets has what he needs in order to be saved—let him hear them. There is no hint here or elsewhere in the Synoptics that a special relation to Jesus is required over and above hearing Moses and the prophets.

There is a remarkable passage in Paul's Corinthian correspondence that counts against particularism in another way.

I want you to know, brethren, that our fathers were all under the cloud, and all passed through the sea, and all were baptized into Moses in the cloud and in the sea, and all ate the same supernatural [or spiritual] food and all drank the same supernatural drink. For they drank from the supernatural Rock which followed them, and the Rock was Christ. Nevertheless, with most of them God was not pleased; for they were overthrown in the wilderness." (1 Cor. 10:1–5)

Paul's concern in this passage is to warn the Corinthian congregation against complacency. They are not to count so heavily on the efficacy of the sacraments of baptism and the Lord's Supper that they assume that nothing evil can happen to them no matter how loosely they behave. In order to support his argument, Paul cites the experience of the Israelites in the wilderness after the exodus from Egypt. Some of those ancestors, in their complacency, fell into idolatry, immorality, and grumbling against God; and the result was that thousands of them were destroyed. Why were they complacent? Like some of the Corinthians, who counted too much on the protection of the sacraments, the ancestors had counted too much on their *equivalents* to the sacraments. This is the interesting part for our purposes. The Israelites, too, had "baptism." They were "baptized" into Moses in the pillar of cloud that guided them and in the sea, when they walked through it as they escaped from Egypt. And the Israelite ancestors had the "Eucharist," too. Their "bread from heaven" was the manna with which God supplied them in the wilderness. Their "supernatural drink," equivalent to the wine and the blood of Christ in the Eucharist, was the water that flowed from the rock when Moses struck it (Exod. 17:6 and Num. 20:7–11). "And the Rock was Christ," said Paul.

For Paul, it was not only true that one and the same God both dealt with the Israelites in the wilderness and dealt with the

Corinthian church in his day. It was also true that *Christ* functioned in both places. How could Christ be present in the days of Moses? For Paul, Christ preexisted his career as Jesus of Nazareth. Christ existed before the creation of the world; God created the world through Christ, "through whom are all things and through whom we exist" (1 Cor. 8:6). Thus for Paul the title "Christ," very much like the title "Word of God" in John, stands for a function of God, God turning toward the world and toward persons, in loving concern, to give revelation of himself and to bring redemption. When God came to Moses and the Israelites, to conduct them through the sea, to guide them through the wilderness, to feed them and to give them drink, that was the Christ-function of God. And when Jesus of Nazareth came, that was the Christ-function of God, too, in the person of Jesus. How much more, for Paul already, the title "Christ" conveys than does the title "Messiah"!

For Paul, everything that he knows both as a Jew and as a Christian comes together in one sacred history. For Christians who know the Hebrew Bible (the Old Testament), a similar thing happens. The whole drama hangs together. The only trouble is that many Christians have unhistorically "Christianized" the Hebrew Bible. Abraham, the model of faith, and Moses, the founder of the nation, and David and Solomon, Amos and Isaiah, Hosea and Jeremiah have all been construed as "Christians before Christ." By the same token they have been de-Judaized; they do not count as Jews and they bring no glory to Judaism. What we can learn from Paul is to see the Jewish sacred history as both *Jewish* and sacred, and beyond that to see it all as informed by the presence of "Christ." The same Christ that Christians worship was and is present in Jewish history under other names. Therefore Jews have had and have the benefit of the Christ-function of God.

The Gospel of John provides a similar scheme for seeing sacred history as one whole. The Gospel opens this way:

In the beginning was the Word, and the Word was with God, and the Word was God. He was in the beginning with God; all things were made through him, and without him was not anything made that was made. In him was life, and the life was the light of men. . . . The true light that enlightens every man was coming into the world. . . . And the Word became flesh and dwelt among us, full of grace and truth. . . . (John 1:1–14)

The Greek word translated as "Word" is *Logos*. It is a word with a marvelously rich history of associations in the ancient world. From the pre-Socratic Greek philosopher Heraclitus down through the Stoics, *Logos* was used as a name for God, with special reference to the rationality of God or the divine Reason with which he made the world. We humans too had been enlightened with the same rationality, by which we were enabled to understand the world and our roles in it under God.

Meanwhile, Jews who were acquainted with Greek thought developed the concept—similar to the *Logos*—of God's Wisdom and almost created a mythology by personifying Wisdom. In the book of Proverbs, Wisdom is presented as saying, "The Lord created me at the beginning of his work, the first of his acts of old. Ages ago I was set up, at the first, before the beginning of the earth. . . . When he established the heavens, I was there, . . . when he marked out the foundations of the earth, then I was beside him, like a master workman; . . . he who finds me finds life and obtains favor from the Lord" (Prov. 8:22–35).

Jews went on to identify Wisdom with the Torah, and attributes were exchanged between them. The Torah, too, was said to have been made before the foundation of the world, and to have assisted God in the creation (Ecclesiasticus 24:8–11, 23; Bar. 3:37–4:1).

The term *Logos* in John seems to gather up all these rich associations: with God's Reason, his Wisdom, his creativity, his concern for humanity's well-being, his will to make himself and his intentions for people known. One's attention is then drawn to the use of the term *Logos* as identification for Jesus. Who *is* this Jesus of Nazareth? How shall we account for his greatness? He is the divine, preexistent *Logos*, the fullness of God's revelation of himself and of his plans for the world, become flesh and blood and dwelling among us.

Not to be overlooked, however, is the broad universalism that characterizes this use of the term *Logos*. Jesus was identified with the cosmic power of enlightenment that had long been familiar in the Greek and Hellenistic worlds. To some extent, it was then being said, the *Logos* that was in Jesus was already known to pagans and had already enlightened them. Pagans were not simply in the dark and damned already. Through the previous work of the *Logos*, pagans already had a lot in common with Christians. So the ground was laid for dialogue and exchange between pagans and Christians.

In a parallel way, by the use of the same term *Logos*, Jesus was suggested to Jewish readers as at one with the preexistent Wisdom and Torah of God. Once again, the effect was anything but particularist. On the one hand, presentation of Jesus as the *Logos* solicited high respect for Jesus among Greek-speaking Jewish readers on the ground that they already revered him as the divine Wisdom. On the other hand, it complimented the same audience by telling them that, far from being in the outer darkness, they were already on good terms with the one who was being presented to them as savior: God's Wisdom (and Torah!) in his incarnation as Jesus. Again, a way was opened for Christians to enter dialogue with non-Christians—in this case Greek-speaking Jews—whom they respected and with whom they knew they had much in common.

What was the purpose of such dialogue? For Paul and for John, the purpose was to convert persons from paganism and Judaism to Christianity. Non-Christians who were encountered on their common ground with Christians were to be brought along until they occupied the distinctively Christian ground as well. Thus Paul hoped that all men including the Jews would come to accept Jesus of Nazareth as the fullness of the eternal Christ.

The purpose of dialogue between Christians and Jews today cannot have this same purpose. For one reason, if Jews are informed that this is its purpose, they will not participate. But there is another better reason: there is no need to convert Jews to Christianity; they are already with the Father. The purpose of the dialogue is to accomplish what has developed in Christian ecumenical dialogue: mutual enrichment. What Christians stand to gain is what the *Logos*, the eternal Christ, has been teaching the Jews all this time.

The story of Franz Rosenzweig suggests a non-particularist way of relating Judaism and Christianity to one another. Rosenzweig was born in 1886 into a German Jewish family that knew itself to be Jewish but had largely ceased to be observant. Eugen Rosenstock-Huessy, a Christain friend, convinced him that religious faith was both possible for an intellectual such as he was and necessary for life. Rosenzweig decided that Christianity was the properly Europeanized and modernized version of Judaism for him to adopt, and he began to make plans to be baptized. But he also felt that it was unbecoming for him to present himself for baptism as a "pagan" and that he ought to come as one who knew what it was to be a Jew. He therefore decided to attend the synagogue and recover himself as a Jew first. By the time he had finished the observance of the Day of Atonement in 1913, he had been converted to Judaism. He gave up the idea of baptism and became a powerful force in a renascence of Jewish education and theology.

Rosenzweig kept up a lifelong interest in Christianity. The position he developed on the interrelationship of Judaism and Christianity makes both necessary in God's plan. The Jew is a member of the "eternal" people which by its life and worship and noninvolvement in the formation of world history witnesses to the eternal God. Christianity is the missionary arm of Judaism, called to bring the word of the Lord to the gentiles, so that ultimately all the ends of the earth will have turned to the one God and been saved. It is quite true, said Rosenzweig, that "no one comes to the Father" but by Jesus. That is, only Jesus and the church are bringing the true God to the nations. However, "the situation is quite different for one who does not have to reach the Father because he is already with him."* The people Israel is already with the Father.

Rosenzweig died in 1929 and a great deal has happened since, particularly of a kind to draw Jews very much into history —the holocaust and the establishment of the state of Israel. Perhaps Rosenzweig would have expressed himself differently today. It may also seem disappointing to some that he made no place for the other living religions of the world. But one thing powerfully commends his formula and that is his Jewish acceptance of Christianity as valid and as part of God's own provision for the world. The long European history of the persecution of Jews in a Christian society did not, at a time when Rosenzweig had strongly identified himself with Judaism, blind him to the continuities between Judaism and Christianity and their complementarity.

What one wants to see is Christians returning the compliment —sufficient Christian openness to the nature of Judaism to recognize that Judaism worships the same God in substantially the same way. The accidents of history are what they are, including the Jewish-Christian rivalry of the past and the mutual exclusion of each other from belonging to the chosen people of God. But when the dust and intemperateness of controversy are allowed to settle, Christians and Jews can embrace each other as younger and older brothers in the same household.

*Nahum N. Glatzer, *Franz Rosenzweig, His Life and Thought* (New York: Schocken Books, 1961), p. 341.

If we can learn to say with Rosenzweig that Christianity is the "Judaism" of the gentiles, perhaps we can also learn to say that Judaism is the "Christianity" of the Jews.

We are brought back to the *covenant* God made with the people Israel. When God called Abraham to leave his father's house and his kinsmen, he promised to make of him a great nation. "And I will bless you," said God, "and make your name great, so that you will be a blessing. I will bless those who bless you, and him who curses you I will curse; and by you all the families of the earth will bless themselves" (Gen. 12:2–3). Later we read that God said to Abraham, "Sarah your wife shall bear you a son, and you shall call his name Isaac. I will establish my covenant with him as an everlasting covenant for his descendants after him" (Gen. 17:19).

In the biblical account of the days of Moses, God was said to have remembered his covenant and therefore to have liberated his people from Egypt (Exod. 2:24). At this point, there was a further explication of the purpose of the covenant. "Now therefore, if you will obey my voice and keep my covenant, . . . you shall be to me a kingdom of priests and a holy nation" (Exod. 19:5–6). Thereupon the covenant was made anew at Mount Sinai; the people accepted its terms as stated in the Ten Commandments and other laws, "and Moses took the blood and threw it upon the people, and said, 'Behold the blood of the covenant which the Lord has made with you in accordance with all these words' " (Exod. 24:8).

At great moments in Israel's history, the covenant was renewed again and again. Joshua both renewed it at Shechem in Canaan and extended it to other tribes who bound themselves to worship the Lord alone (Josh. 24:19–28). King Josiah renewed it for himself and his people at Jerusalem in the seventh century, accepting the core of the book of Deuteronomy as the authoritative statement of the people's obligations. Ezra in the fifth century presided at another covenant-renewal in which the Pentateuch, probably in the very form in which we have it, became the definition of God's requirements.

In the background of this latest renewal of the covenant stood the great words of the Second Isaiah, in which what it means to be a kingdom of priests and a holy nation achieved further definition. "I will give you as a light to the nations, that my salvation may reach to the end of the earth" (Isa. 49:6).

We have in these texts and others like them the meaning of being "chosen people" and the meaning of the "election of Israel." God had singled out one people, but not out of mere favoritism and not for preferential treatment or indulgence. As Amos the prophet said, the special relationship of Israel to God meant that God expected more, not less, of his people, and it would go harder with them than with others when they disappointed him (Amos 3:2). But beyond that, it was for the sake of the well-being of all humanity that God had chosen Israel: they were to be God's priest and prophet, to bring to all nations the truth about the one God and about his intentions and expectations for all.

There is not a word in the scripture to say that God has changed his mind. Even when Israel was seen by the prophets to be most disobedient to God and most exposed to his judgment and even about to be decimated, there was always in their minds the notion of "the remnant," those survivors with whom God would remain in covenant and through whom he would pursue his purposes. Even when Jeremiah, in the face of defiance of his preaching and the collapse of his people's independence, foretold a day when God would make a "new covenant," it was in his mind still to be a "covenant with the house of Israel and the house of Judah" (Jer. 31:31).

How did Jews fulfill their calling to be a light to the nations? By worship, by obedience to God's law, by public service, by works of lovingkindness, by martyrdom, even by missionary proclamation. In the centuries immediately before and after the time of Jesus, Jews were ardent missionaries. They attracted many "God-fearers," who attended the synagogues and worshiped the one God without becoming Jews, and many converts. But they were forced to give up making converts, first temporarily by the pagan Roman emperor Hadrian, then more permanently by the Christian Roman empire. Perhaps, when the Middle Ages made Jewish life utterly precarious, they lost the heart to invite gentiles to accept the risks of being Jewish. Furthermore, they could console themselves in a quiet, non-proselytizing kind of witnessing to the God of righteousness by knowing, as the Talmud taught, that the righteous of all nations have a share in the world to come.

It is true that some early Christians announced that they were the new and true Israel, and that the fall of Jerusalem in A.D. 70 was the sign of God's rejection of the old Israel. But that was one opinion, given in the heat of controversy. Jews of the time also accepted the fall of Jerusalem as a judgment of God, as they had accepted everything else in history. But God's judgment was not God's rejection, and they went on faithfully thinking about what they had to learn from it, but never doubting the covenant itself. When Franz Rosenzweig went to the synagogue on the Day of Atonement, perhaps for the first time in his life at age twenty-seven, and felt the power of that liturgy by which he was summoned to present himself and all his sins to the living God and to be forgiven, he knew that the covenant was still in effect. He knew what it was to be with the Father. And a Christian who has come to the same Father and trembled in the same way can know that he was right.

The "People of God" is at least large enough to contain all Jews and all Christians.

6

ISRAEL

We have paid considerable attention to similarities between Judaism and Christianity out of concern to demonstrate to Christians how much of what they regard as religiously valid is a common possession of both faiths. What Jews and Christians share is a basis for mutual recognition of each other's religious legitimacy and beyond that a basis for fellowship.

There are some important differences between Judaism and Christianity, too. These should also be discussed in order that they may be understood positively and not taken as barriers to fellowship. These differences have their own legitimacy in view of the differing historical experiences of the two faith-communities.

One of these differences on the Jewish side and perhaps the most important is Jewish peoplehood. Its most familiar aspect is that a person is born a Jew. Far back in the days of Moses and Joshua, Jews acquired nationhood almost simultaneously with acquiring their religion. For centuries, to be a member of the nation, living in its territory, was the only way to be included in the roll of the congregation. The Babylonian captivity in the sixth century B.C. taught Jews the art of maintaining their religious identity in a foreign land, and it included the art of maintaining their national identity, so that when the chance came they went home to Jerusalem again in an effort to rebuild a national existence.

Diaspora (dispersion) or *Galut* (exile) is the way Jews have characterized their existence ever since the fall of Jerusalem to the Romans in A.D. 70. That is, wherever they lived outside the Holy Land, they were conscious of living away from home, away from where they belonged. This is symbolized in the annual repetition of the wish incorporated in the liturgy of the *Seder*, "Next year in Jerusalem!" In the *Galut*, Jews have lived the life of exiles for most of the last nineteen hundred years. Not until the time of the French Revolution was a Jew ever a *citizen* of a European country. Before that, he was a resident alien of Jewish nationality—a member of a nation within the nation and yet also a stateless person—who lived in his own quarter much as in a ghetto and was governed according to his own laws by his own rabbis and elders. His laws and customs —*kashrut* and Sabbath-observance, for example—were so distinctive that he was a decided foreigner anywhere else in the host land and only secure among his own people—except that his whole commmunity was made insecure repeatedly. In such a world, to grow up a Jew was to grow up in so thoroughly Jewish a religious environment that there was only one religious option—Talmudic Judaism. Peoplehood perpetuated the religion. But even more, Judaic religion, which was not merely doctrine but the *complete* definition of the Jewish way of life, perpetuated peoplehood.

Since the French Revolution and the varying degrees of cultural assimilation of Jews that citizenship brought in its train, the situation has changed somewhat. A Jew like Franz Rosenzweig grew up at the end of the nineteenth century with a very dilute sense of belonging to a people and with numerous religious options, Jewish as well as Christian and agnostic. Such

Jews styled themselves Europeans of the Jewish persuasion and were opposed to Zionism, thinking of it as nationalistic but not religious. There has been a tremendous revival of the sense of peoplehood since Rosenzweig's youth; furthermore, it would still have to be said today that one is born a Jew as a matter of peoplehood, *with a good chance* of being converted to Judaism. A Jew who totally fails to be converted to Judaism tends to disappear from the ranks of the people, unless a Hitler forces him back into the ranks on purely ethnic grounds. Even so, his membership in the Jewish people keeps exposing him to Jewish religion, and the possibility that he will be converted to Judaism continues. So it remains true today that the religion of Judaism creates a distinctive people, the Jews, so much so that without the religion the people would disappear; and it remains true that the people, with all its distinctive culture, which is saturated with religious meanings, perpetuates Judaism.

Christians have experienced just enough of ethnically oriented denominationalism to be able to understand Jewish peoplehood. However, Christians cannot, by transcending their own ethnicity, attain a position from which they can authoritatively inform Jews that religion and ethnicity are two distinct things that have no necessary connection with each other. It is simply a fact that for Jews peoplehood and religion are intertwined and interdependent. As Simon Dubnow asserted, the Jews have been a "spiritual nation" for nineteen hundred years—that is, a nation without political existence but a nation nonetheless, carrying with it a religious, moral, and legal constitution which sustained it and gave it character.

The peoplehood of Jews goes far to explain the modern state of Israel. First of all, as we have seen, Jews with their strong sense of living in exile perpetuated their people's love affair with the Holy Land and their sense that one day they would be reunited there. Praying facing in the direction of Jerusalem, with a religious picture placed to represent the direction, was a symbol of this. The Messianic hope, too, included the element that the Messiah would reign from Jerusalem and that his people would be gathered to him there. And the people prayed, in the words of the *Kaddish*, "May he establish his kingdom during your lifetime and days and during the lifetime of the whole house of Israel, speedily and soon." Ah, perhaps it would be "next year in Jerusalem"!

In modern times the traditional longing to return was rethought, as a result of antisemitic persecutions and with a new sense of its feasibility. In the midst of persecutions in Russia in the 1880's various rabbis began to say that it was not necessary to wait for the days of the Messiah; moving to Palestine to await him might even hasten his coming. In twenty years, twenty-five thousand Russian Jews emigrated to colonize there. Another Russian Jew, Ahad Ha-Am, urged colonization of Palestine in the name of "cultural Zionism." He argued that one place in the world where Jews were a majority and could produce their own cultural and religious expression without hindrance would be an inspiration and reinforcement of Jewish life everywhere.

Theodor Herzl, the founder of political Zionism with his book *The Jewish State* in 1896 and his convocation of the first World Zionist Congress in 1897, was driven by his conviction that Jews would be safe from persecution nowhere but in a land of their own. What moved Herzl was his covering of the Dreyfus trial for a Vienna newspaper. Alfred Dreyfus, a Jew and a captain in the French army, was framed by the perpetrators of a sale of French military secrets to appear to be guilty in their stead. He was tried, found guilty, and sent to Devil's Island. When members of the French press and literary figures such as Emile Zola took up his cause, the case was reopened and Dreyfus was eventually exonerated when the guilty were found. What Herzl learned from the events was that if a Captain Dreyfus, because he was a Jew, could successfully be used as a scapegoat in the France that had originated democratic citizenship for European Jews, then Jews were not to assume that they were safe anywhere in Europe. Herzl himself was too secularist to care where the homeland would be located. But once a Jewish state became to Jews an idea whose time had come, the overwhelming majority knew that there was only one place where it could be built—Zion itself, Jerusalem, the Holy Land.

Meanwhile colonization continued as Jewish organizations were able to raise funds in order to purchase land and to finance immigration and cultivation of oranges, grapes, and the like. In 1917 the British government, by means of the Balfour Declaration, promised to work for the establishment of a Jewish national homeland in Palestine. However, after the war the British retreated from the Declaration out of deference to Arab protests. And when Hitler came to power and began to implement his antisemitic policy, there was hardly more readiness to receive Jews in British Mandatory Palestine than in other countries.

In 1947 the United Nations voted to divide the territory of Palestine between Jews and Palestinian Arabs and in 1948 the Jewish state of Israel was proclaimed. In the years since, despite frequent border clashes and full-scale wars with neighboring Arab nations, Israel has proved itself a viable, democratic state, with tremendous energy for scientific research, education, land reclamation and development, irrigation, reforestation, and development of industry. According to the Law of Return, any Jew anywhere in the world has a right to live in Israel and becomes a citizen as soon as he immigrates.

So the state of Israel is an internationally legitimated reality, the joint product of the perennial longing for the land on the part of a spiritual nation-in-exile and of antisemitic persecutions, above all the holocaust.

The state of Israel has been likened in Jewish thought and feeling to the restoration of Judah after the Babylonian captivity. During that captivity Ezekiel had heard the Lord raise the question that all loyal Jews must have felt: "Can these bones live?" Then the Lord answered his own question and said to Ezekiel, "Prophesy to these bones, and say to them, O dry bones, hear the word of the Lord. Thus says the Lord God to these bones: Behold, I will cause breath to enter you, and you shall live" (Ezek. 37:4-5). The Lord continued, "Son of man, these bones are the whole house of Israel. Behold, they say, 'Our bones are dried up, and our hope is lost; we are clean cut off.' Therefore prophesy, and say to them, Thus says the Lord God: Behold I will open your graves, and raise you from your graves, O my people; and I will bring you home into the land of Israel. And you shall know that I am the Lord . . ." (Ezek. 37:11-13). No wonder the birth of the state of Israel has been likened to resurrection after the death of the holocaust.

This high, Ezekiel-like view of the meaning of the state of Israel has not been shared by all Jews. A minority within Orthodox Judaism including some who reside in Israel itself has maintained one kind of religious objection to the reestablishment of the state. For them, there is no divine promise of the restoration of the nation to its homeland apart from the promise of the coming of the days of the Messiah. To bring the Messiah is strictly God's prerogative. Therefore creating the state by human political means was an arrogant effort to force God's hand and cannot be expected to have God's blessing. Simultaneously a minority in the community of Reform Judaism, expressing itself through the American Council for Judaism, has been opposed to any sort of revival of Jewish nationalism and nationality, on the grounds that the diaspora is the normal space of modern Jewish existence and that Jewishness is purely a religious commitment (in the manner in which Christianity is), to be fulfilled wherever one finds onself. Somewhat akin to both these positions is another Jewish point of view that has come to expression more recently. It deplores what it sees as a tendency to reduce Judaism to Zionism, to lose the eschatological dimension of Jewish faith altogether in the assumption that the state of Israel represents fulfilled messianism, and to sacrifice all other Jewish concerns to the well-being of the state of Israel.

If Jews indicate some confusion about the meaning to them of the state of Israel, it is natural that Christians exhibit much more confusion. There are some items, however, on which Christians probably can agree.

1. One of these is that the state of Israel is a legitimate state. Its territory is essentially that of the ancient state of Israel, a territory continuously lived in by descendants of Abraham from patriarchal times to the present. Much more, the modern state of Israel has the legitimacy of having been chartered by the United Nations, in one of its few actions in which both the U.S.S.R. and the U.S.A. expressly concurred.

2. The state of Israel is for Jews a *necessary* alternative to the diaspora. Jews who prefer living in the diaspora should of course be absolutely free to do so and secure in doing so. The diaspora, especially in the United States, offers access to unexcelled opportunities in education, the arts, the sciences, industry, and technology. However, there are other places where Jews have found themselves in recent years, in Europe, in North Africa, and in the Middle East, where life has been bleak or dangerous or both. If we consider the quota restrictions that operate against Jews who desire to emigrate from these places, it is a necessity of life that there be one place where Jews are always welcome to settle. Israel is that one place.

3. The world of nations must find a way of guaranteeing that living in Israel will not be equivalent to victimization in another holocaust. Israel is not only necessary and legitimate—it is also in being, the home of two and a half million Jewish men, women, and children. The danger lies in the neighboring governments that have not accepted Israel's legitimacy and have in addition pledged to drive the Israelis into the sea. There is no

inherent impossibility of achieving their acceptance of Israel's existence and of its eventual boundaries. Hundreds of thousands of Christian and Muslim Arabs get along well with Israeli Jews as fellow-citizens of Israel. With its technical proficiencies, Israel could be a strong stimulus to economic development of the Middle East. What is required to make this achievement possible in the long run are international guarantees of Israel's survival and sovereignty in the meantime.

It goes without saying that Christians who see the urgency of these three items find themselves in agreement on these same matters with the vast majority of American Jews. This does not mean, however, that there are no strains in Jewish-Christian relations because of Israel. Some Christians have felt that nothing less than their full endorsement of every element of Israeli policy, domestic and foreign, would be enough to satisfy their Jewish friends. On the other hand, when the state of Israel is severely threatened not only with defeat but with extinction, as it was in the Six Days' War in 1967 and the October War of 1973, and another holocaust seems to be in the making, Jews cannot understand the failure of Christian friends and spokesmen to cry out and act in support of Israel.

Christians also need to be careful not to make demands of the state of Israel, because of its name and connection with Jewish religion, that are unrealistic to make of any nation. It is true that much religious idealism and political utopianism went into the founding of Israel. The Messianic element in Zionism fostered dreams of the perfectly just society, the perfectly Torah-true community. But it is naive to expect realization of such dreams. State power is constantly confronted with morally ambiguous choices even when it is not surrounded by armed enemies and terrorists; therefore no state can be expected to be righteous, especially by persons who know that not even any person can be righteous.

There is no simple formula for the resolution of the problems here. But the tensions can be reduced once Christians have the habit of seeing Jews as fellow-members of the People of God and of exposing themselves to Jewish at least as much as to contrary perspectives.

Christians have sometimes heard the issue of dual citizenship raised against Jews. That is, how can Jews be loyal simultaneously to Israel and to the country of their legal citizenship, for example, the United States? What if the interests of the two nations diverge? Jews regard this as a pseudo-problem, and so should Christians. A Jewish citizen of the United States has only one citizenship and one citizen-loyalty, to the United States. He takes pride in Israel as a progressive democracy and as a refuge for Jews who may be under attack or under threat anywhere in the world. It is also an exciting place to visit, but he would not want to live there.

Christians may need to prepare themselves also for encountering Jewish views of Jesus. There is a sense in which the fears previously ascribed to Luther, that Christian mistreatment of Jews gave Jesus himself a bad name among Jews, were justified, especially in earlier times. But there is hardly any such danger today, not because Christian abuse of Jews has disappeared, but because the Jewish community in the United States and in Israel is sophisticated with reference to its own history. Jesus is a part of that history. He is a Jew in whom Jews take pride. As a teacher, he pointed precisely to what Jews believe is the essence of their law, love for God and love for man. As the crucified, he died resolutely as one who would not abandon his teaching for fear or favor. In view of the great spiritual and moral wealth that has flowed from him through the church into the countless gentiles who have believed in him, he is one of the supreme Jewish benefactors of humanity.

Of course Jesus is to Jews fully human, not divine. Given the Jewish sense of God and of the world, it is simply not thinkable that there could be anyone who was both God and man. It required the thorough immersion of Christianity in Hellenistic ways of thought to make the Trinitarian formulas possible. Among Jews, even the Messiah and the Son of Man were always altogether human. The Messiah was in a way called "Son of God" in Psalm 2, as we saw, when the Lord God was pictured as saying to him, "You are my son, today I have begotten you" (Ps. 2:7). But that was an honorary title, implying that God had adopted him as his ward and beneficiary for the well-being of the people. When Jews did develop, in Hellenistic times, the idea of a preexistent, supernatural Wisdom, the created "daughter" of God who worked with God in the creation of the world, they never contemplated the incarnation of Wisdom in a human being. Thus Jewish belief that Jesus is fully human is the natural, good-faith consequence of their view of God.

7

AGENDA

Let us assume that the argument developed in this essay is on the whole correct: that Jews and Christians are variations on one theme. Judaism and Christianity are alternative developments of one religious tradition, the tradition that produced the Hebrew Bible. Both faiths worship the same God. Both share a common scripture, the Hebrew Bible. Both pray in parallel language— and at times identical language (the psalms)—for the coming of the kingdom of God. The better the adherents of the two faiths come to know each other, the more they see how much they have in common; for just about every feature in either religion, the other has an equivalent. Christianity can be seen as "Judaism" made available to gentiles. Judaism can be seen as the "new covenant" of the Jews. Christians can look at Jews and say, "They are really very much like us—they are Christians, in a sense." Jews can look at Christians and say, "They are really very much like us—they are Jews, in a sense."

Let us assume not only that Judaism and Christianity are variations on one theme but that Jews and Christians will both be the gainers for recognizing this. Both will give up wasting energy committed to perpetuating rivalry. Both will be enriched by sharing each other's insights into common possessions of the greatest importance. How then is this recognition of standing within the same covenant-relationship with God to be made more available? How is this recognition to be acted out, even institutionalized, so that it becomes normative for future generations?

Each of us who has a church or synagogue relationship is in touch with two or three levels of religious organization through which new concepts and programs can be established. One of these is the local congregation; another is the denominational headquarters which both supervises and provides service to local congregations. A third level is represented by intermediate (such as regional) jurisdictions and by religious service organizations for men, women, youth, and special programs. Still another level is represented by the National Council of the Churches of Christ in the U.S.A. and by the Synagogue Council of America, each of which has programs in the area of interreligious relationships. These federations are service organizations to which the denominations surrender none of their sovereignty, but which enable Christian and Jewish denominations respectively to speak with a common voice from time to time and to undertake certain kinds of common work together.

The National Conference of Christians and Jews is an autonomous organization; its primary focus is to encourage dialogue between churches and synagogues and to convene study groups on a regional and national basis to work on problems in Jewish-Christian understanding, such as the status of the state of Israel.

What can and ought to be done on the denominational level and the level of federations of denominations?

1. Denominations frequently have theological study groups, either on a standing or *ad hoc* basis, that investigate emerging concerns. Such groups prepare documents that enable the denomination to articulate its position on a problem, for example, abortion. Or study booklets may be prepared for the consti-

tuency of the denomination, so that members may draw their own conclusions and make up their own minds with the benefit of expert assistance. Would it not be well if Christian and Jewish denominations and federations commissioned such study groups now to explore the question, "Who are we Christians and Jews to each other?"

2. A primary consequence of the work of such study groups might very well be the explicit denial by Christian denominations of any need for Jews to become Christians in order to be saved and the express renunciation of Christian missionary efforts directed toward the conversion of Jews. As we have seen, Christians can believe that Jews "are with the Father" and have all the resources they need for salvation within their own covenant and tradition. In fact, must we not conclude that Christians in positions of denominational leadership *already do believe this*? If the contrary were true, if denominational leaders believed that Jews were lost or damned as Jews, would they not be under obligation to do all that is in their power to bring Jews to saving faith in Jesus as the Christ? Would they not be committed to developing the strategies, the funding, the literature, and the personnel for a successful mission to Jews? Would not every congregation be urged to have a committee on evangelization of the Jews? Would not the books of liturgy provide weekly prayers for the conversion of the Jews? Would it not be a well-publicized ideal in the churches to motivate and train every Christian to take part in a missionary approach to Jews that would be conducted here at home, where one lives and where one works? But none of these basic elements of a church mission for proselytizing the Jews is in place. Why? Is this because church leaders believe that Jews are not lost as Jews? Is this because Christian leaders know that God's ancient people are still God's people? But this knowledge has never been made articulate. It has never been shared with the membership of the

churches. Is it not high time now to make this judgment explicit and clear to Christians and Jews?

Jews have no need to make an equivalent statement from their side, because it has been their historic position that the righteous of all nations have a share in the world to come. Thus they never proclaimed that a person had to be a Jew to be saved. But Christianity has identified itself historically with the particularist position.

There are two good reasons to want the Christian denominations to renounce proselytization of Jews as promptly as possible. One is that as long as proselytization is not renounced Jews expect that it is still intended. The interchurch "Key 73" program of 1973, which proposed "to win the continent for Christ," made many American Jews extraordinarily nervous. Rightly or wrongly, they felt directly targeted, and they are well aware, as we have seen, that when they are the objects of evangelization they run added risks of being exposed to resentment and hostility.

The other reason to wish to see the Christian denominations renounce proselytization of the Jews is that proselytization plays into the hands of antisemitism. For to proselytize Jews is to assert that a Jew must be converted in order to be saved; this in turn is to assert that he stands rejected by God as he is, as a Jew, and revives the connected notions that God rejected the Jews as Jews because of their rejection of Jesus, and that Jews are under the wrath of God until they accept Jesus as "the True Savior." These beliefs about rejection and wrath demonstrably feed antisemitism.

3. Denominational study groups that would explore the nature of Judaism and the interconnectedness of Judaism and Christianity and would articulate the validity of the Jewish covenant with the Father would find it very natural to lead the way for denominations to combat antisemitism actively. As we have

seen on earlier pages, antisemitism must be taken very seriously in view of its power to produce the torture-murders of six million men, women, and children in Nazi Europe. In addition, Christians must take antisemitism very seriously as a specifically Christian sin, in view of the evidence that a certain way of telling the Christian story rationalizes antisemitism, that is, makes it appear rational and proper. Christians are therefore called upon to rid themselves of antisemitism and to help the world to rid itself of antisemitism. That is, Christians *ought* to be called upon to do so. But who—what human voices—are actually calling upon Christians to be rid of antisemitism? Recent events "call upon Christians" to purge themselves; but these events do *not* call Christians audibly unless they are interpreted by human beings.

The Christian denominations have an immense task here. Some have adopted statements condemning antisemitism; the Roman Catholic bishops at Vatican Council II and numerous Protestant groups have done this. But much more needs to be done. Denominations have many channels of communication with their constituencies: pastoral letters, official magazines, statements by leaders, curriculum materials for children, youth, and men's and women's societies, church bulletin covers, devotional booklets, and many more. In view of the holocaust does anyone feel that his denomination has denounced antisemitism loudly enough, often enough, effectively enough? Have the denominational media really been exploited in this cause? Have Christians been sufficiently led in acts of repentance for the antisemitism that has characterized the church?

Furthermore, it is not only not enough for each denomination to deliver a condemnation of antisemitism once and to make one public statement of repentance for the Christian antisemitism of the past; Christians at all levels of responsibility should attack current expressions of antisemitism. Clearly, when the antisemitic offense is at the national level, action should come from

Christian denominations and the National Council of Churches, too, and not only the Jewish service organizations such as the Anti-Defamation League of B'nai B'rith and the American Jewish Committee, and the independent National Conference of Christians and Jews.

4. Parallel to denominational study groups are teams of theologians and leaders who represent their denominations in dialogue with similar teams representing other denominations. The objectives sought in such dialogues are joint statements in which the constituencies are informed as to the area of agreement achieved. Anglican and Roman Catholic teams have published agreements about the meaning of the Eucharist. Roman Catholic and Lutheran groups have been able to arrive at some agreements about justification and about the Papacy. Dialogues between Jewish and various Christian denominational representatives have also been conducted. In the nature of the case, these conversations begin "farther back," at more elementary levels. No agreements on theological questions have yet been attempted. But after expressing satisfaction that a beginning has been made, ought not one to urge that the frequency and scope of such conversations be greatly increased?

Dialogues between Christian and Jewish leaders will be helpful in connection with two Christian projects mentioned above, that is, working out the theology of reconciliation between Christians and Jews as fellow-worshipers of one God and developing an adequate strategy for getting rid of Christian antisemitism. In fact, it would seem that neither project can be carried out properly without constant reference to Jewish experience and Jewish opinion.

There are a number of other kinds of objectives that can be sought in Jewish-Christian dialogue, all of which seem important. One type of aim relates to discovering areas for common action of an educational or political nature. The United States seems on the whole to be well committed to religious pluralism, no religious community enjoying any favors from government or society that are not available to all. But if there are infringements of religious liberty, how much better if Christians and Jews come forward to deal with them together in common cause! But this will only be possible if Christians and Jews have previously agreed on the moral basis for common action and on the mechanisms by which it is to be set in motion. The case is very similar for any public question that is essentially a moral question—for example, developing legislation in regard to divorce, or abortion, or housing, or environmental pollution, or poverty, or expressions of racism. If Jews and Christians can be associated in common action in many such instances, their causes will be strengthened and in addition they will have proclaimed something valuable about who Christians and Jews are to one another.

Still another area to be explored in dialogue is that typified by such a matter as Jewish-Christian intermarriage. Understanding the small numbers of Jews, the rarity of conversions to Judaism, and the dependence of Judaism on its constituents' sense of peoplehood, we are not surprised that Jewish leaders feel threatened by the frequency of Jewish marriages into other faith-communities. Rabbinical groups forbid their members to officiate at such weddings. Is it possible that dialogue between Jewish and Christian leaders will be able to bring any comfort in this area, so that what appear to be losses to one or the other of the religious communities may be regarded as gains in another way? There are grounds for arguing that some of the best interpreters of Judaism to Christians and reconcilers of the two faiths have been Christians of Jewish descent.

It is still a fact, as we have noted, that Jewish religion is geared to deeds more than to theology. Dialogue-teams representing Jews can be counted on to be very much interested in moral issues and in programs of social action. They can be expected to be less interested in discussing theology, at least at the beginning. But as Jewish-Christian dialogues progress and build up mutual confidence, the time will come when they can enter upon the discussion of theological questions, for example, the nature of God and of his participation in history. When that day comes, the day of mutual theological stimulation and enrichment will also come.

5. The various Christian and Jewish denominations are related in various ways to institutions of higher learning: colleges, universities, and theological seminaries. They are therefore able to do certain things on the campus to strengthen ties between Christians and Jews. Much has already been done in this area through the teaching of the scriptures in the light of the higher criticism and the more objective presentation of church history. Thus the Glock and Stark study shows that the more educated the members of the church constituency are, the less they are characterized by religious prejudice. Nevertheless, there is more to be done here, too, perhaps most of all in the seminaries. Another study in which Glock and Stark participated,[*] indicates that the Christian clergy are not so much saying the right things about Jews and not being believed as they are saying wrong things and being believed. If the denominations are going to work toward a theology of reconciliation between Judaism and Christianity and develop the rationale and strategy for eliminating Christian antisemitism, their seminaries are of critical importance. The seminary faculties are on the whole the clergy who are best equipped to serve on theological task forces. The seminaries themselves are theological laboratories where ideas and techniques can be experimented with. And the human products of the seminaries, the next generations of clergy, can carry out to their parishes a wholly new attitude toward Jews and new wisdom about the place of Judaism in God's plan of salvation.

---

[*]Rodney Stark, Bruce D. Foster, Charles Y. Glock, and Harold E. Quinley, *Wayward Shepherds* (New York: Harper & Row, 1971).

The actual curricular changes to be introduced may be of two kinds. One is a more positive and appreciative treatment of Judaism wherever it is encountered in the traditional curriculum, particularly in the study of the Hebrew Bible, the intertestamental period, the New Testament, and church history. The other is the offering of courses directly focused on Judaism, particularly those aspects of it that throw light on the meaning of the Christian heritage, such as Jewish liturgy, theology, biblical and legal interpretation, mysticism, and spirituality. It is likely that precisely those studies that show the Christian debt to Judaism will be the ones that will endear Judaism to Christian students.

The seminaries or theological study groups can also explore and suggest ways in which the Christian clergy can relate themselves and their congregations to Jewish congregations in their neighborhoods.

6. The Christian and Jewish denominations all engage in preparing instructional materials for use in their local congregations by children and adults. The purpose of these materials is to provide for the education of the laity in the faith and traditions of the religious community. Many denominations assume that these materials are taught by lay teachers without extensive theological training, and therefore the materials usually are accompanied by teachers' guides including considerable amounts of background information and much specific advice as to the objectives to be sought and the methods that may be used. In short, the denominations accept a large measure of responsibility for the impact of their curricula. For this reason there has been much interest in recent years as to how such Christian curricula have dealt with Jews and Judaism.

Bernhard Olson made a classic study in this area.* Olson organized the theological spectrum of Protestant parish teaching

*Bernhard Olson, *Faith and Prejudice* (New Haven: Yale University Press, 1963).

into four subdivisions: fundamentalist, conservative, neo-ortho-dox, and liberal. He then selected a body of curriculum materi-als representative of each of these perspectives and subjected the materials to careful analysis of the manner in which Jews and Judaism were presented. The results were disturbing to Chris-tians and Jews, because they made it very evident how, in some of these materials, negative images of the Jews could be promul-gated in the very process of fostering development in Christian conviction. (For example, Jews were pictured as opposed to Jesus and thus opposed to God.)

Olson's work was taken with appropriate seriousness, and publications of new denominational curricula since his study are reportedly greatly improved. However, in at least one of these newer curricula there is still much to be desired.* That is to say, there are very few sins of commission, and they are relatively minor. In one case the Pharisees are brought into the story of the plotting against Jesus' life peripherally, but in a way that the Synoptic Gospels do not at all support. In another instance the Pharisees are subjected to the familiar "cheap shot" that they were legalists and therefore had no sense of the weighty as over against the trivial elements of the law.

But what seems much more regrettable are sins of omission. We have seen earlier in this study how deeply indebted Christi-anity is to Judaism: for Jesus, the apostles, the Hebrew Bible. We have noted how Christians tend to conceal this debt by treat-ing the Hebrew heroes as "Christians before Christ." We have considered the Christian guilt in the long centuries of persecu-tions of Jews in Christian lands. Now would Christians like to be a part of a process of righting the balance? Do Christians who regret the centuries of antisemitism now want to develop a Christian philosemitism? Do they now want to give the credit

---

*A follow-up of Olson's study, *Portrait of the Elder Brother* by Gerald S. Strober (New York: The American Jewish Committee and the National Conference of Christians and Jews, 1972) indicates that the inadequacy of this one curriculum is unfortunately still typical.

and the praise to Judaism for all the good Jewish elements that Jesus built into Christianity? What will be involved is much more than giving up misusing Judaism as a foil against which to display the superiority of Christianity—and much more than acknowledging the debt of Christianity to Judaism by "baptizing" the Hebrew Bible as the Christian Old Testament. It will take conscious and conscientious pointing out the innumerable instances in which Judaism has appreciated and preserved and still celebrates the very elements of the biblical tradition in which Christianity most rejoices.

The more the Christian and Jewish denominations will be in dialogue with each other, the more they will want to see to it that the instructional materials on which their laity are being brought up will incorporate the friendliness and mutual concern that feature the dialogues.

7. Another area of responsibility of the denominations, Jewish and Christian, is the preparation and publication of books of liturgy. These prayer books are immensely influential. The constant repetition of the same prayers and psalms burns their phrases and formulas deep into the mind, so that in times of crisis and of meditation they assert themselves as comfort and guidance. The prayerbook too needs to be considered in any effort to foster a new kind of Christian consciousness of Jews.

There are three ways in which prayer books relate to our present concern: they provide calendars of commemoration and observance; they provide scripture readings for Sabbaths or Sundays and special occasions; and they provide the texts of numerous prayers for holy days and weekdays.

In times when the conversion of Jews to Christianity was more on churchmen's minds than it is today, no doubt there were many more prayers in the Christian liturgies for the conversion of the Jews. Today there do not appear to be many. Perhaps the study groups and the dialogue teams will bring us to the point where there will be none. But instead of simply dropping the Jews out of sight during prayers, the denominations should prepare new prayers in which the Jews are prayed for as the branches of the church are prayed for, namely, that God will keep us all and that we will all be drawn closer together in his service. New editions of Christian prayer books might also very well include a fairly large number of prayers from the Jewish prayer book, citing the source. This will be very convenient for common prayers when Jewish groups are present in the church. It will also tend to make the Christian laity familiar with another aspect of Judaism with which they will feel very much at home.

Not all denominations provide lectionaries or tables of scripture readings specified for every Sabbath or Sunday and every special day in the year, but most including the Jewish do. These lectionaries commend themselves in that they provide for the congregations a balanced hearing, in the course of a year of worship, of their most important scriptures. In many Christian communions, however, they mandate the reading of certain passages in the New Testament that can provoke the hearer against the Jews or that present a very particularist version of Christian claims. The denominations for which this problem exists may need to have their attention drawn to two remedies. One remedy would be to revise the lectionary to replace the provocative passages. This is relatively easy to do. Whether the lesson is from the history of the Passion of Jesus or from another place, it is usually possible to find an equivalent portion that does not contain what sounds like an attack on the Jews. The other possible remedy, if the first one proves impracticable, is to provide footnotes for the awkward passages when they are published. Each footnote can suggest what would need to be said in connection with the public reading of the passage in order to prevent the hearers from drawing antisemitic inferences.

Prayer books also provide calendars of days of commemoration, and here too the Christians have followed the Jews. The very style of commemoration has been taken over. When a Christian observes Good Friday, he is helped to place himself at the foot of the cross and to note the resemblance or identity between his sins and the sins that produced the crucifixion. Thus he is helped to repent and so to be forgiven. When a Jew observes Passover, he is helped to place himself among those who were in bondage in Egypt, so that when he celebrates the exodus and the liberation he knows that it was his exodus and his liberation as well. There is now a new day of remembrance in the Jewish calendar, and the Christian denominations may want to add it to their sacred year too. It is *Yom ha-Sho'ah*, the Day of the Holocaust. It is a day for remembering the six million and for letting the horror of their fate question us again and again year after year. Why did they have to die? How well are we assured that no such thing will be permitted to happen again? Have we rid ourselves of any antisemitism that was in us? Have we helped the world to be cured of its antisemitism? To place *Yom ha-Sho'ah* in Christian liturgical calendars would strongly suggest that congregations grapple with the memory of the holocaust at least once every year and draw what conclusions they must. The Christian denominations might also suggest that services on the day include the Jewish prayer called the *Kaddish*. This is also known as the "mourners' prayer" and is prayed daily by the surviving family for eleven months after the death of a loved one and then on the anniversary of the death. Far from being a prayer in which the mourners are led to pity themselves in their grief or to pity the deceased relative, it is a prayer for the coming of God's kingdom and the redemption of all the children of men.

The denominations are expected to and they do offer spiritual, moral, and material leadership and resources to their congregations, and we have been asking ourselves what they can do to improve Christian-Jewish relations. We may also bear in mind that they are the "servants of the servants of God," and that they may require prodding from the servants of God as to what the service of God requires in our time. Every servant of God may have an effect on his denomination, just as every citizen may have an effect on his government. The situation is bound to vary from denomination to denomination, for there are different polities, and it is difficult to predict how much influence a person may have on his denomination by acting as an individual directly. But that leads us to a consideration of what may be accomplished in the local congregation, as well as through the local congregation and intermediate jurisdictions in effecting change at the denomination level.

It would be natural for local congregations of Christians and Jews that desire to improve relations between their faith-communities to begin in more informal ways than would the denominations. However, in some cases, face-to-face social contacts may be impossible or at best difficult to arrange. Jews are not numerous, and they are not evenly distributed throughout the country. Jews in the United States number approximately six million. If they were ranked on a scale with the Christian denominations, they would show up between the Lutherans and the Presbyterians. They are vastly outnumbered by Roman Catholics, outnumbered by Baptists, Methodists, and Lutherans, and they are more numerous than Presbyterians, Episcopalians, members of the United Church of Christ, and the other Christian denominations, taken separately. Thus it is likely that there are many American communities and perhaps even counties in which there is no synagogue at all.

Nevertheless, what may be done in communities in which there is a synagogue (or temple)? Let us begin by assuming that Christians will provide the initiatives. Generally speaking, the Jews are the injured party; Christians are properly the suppliants who feel that it is their place to act first to restore and to further good relations.

If there are Jews in the community, members of the Christian congregations will have friends and acquaintances among them. Let us suppose a Christian begins to talk to Jewish friends about what might be done to encourage some fellowship between his congregation and the synagogue. What are the possibilities?

1. An exchange of visits may be arranged between the two congregations. The hours of worship do not conflict. An obvious occasion for a visit to a synagogue would be a festival day to which Christians already relate, such as Passover (*Pesach*); *Shavuot* (Pentecost), the Feast of Weeks, commemorating the experience at Mount Sinai; or *Sukkot* (Tabernacles), commemorating the wilderness wandering. Some synagogues are already in the habit of inviting Christian friends to participate in a congregational *Seder*, commemorating the exodus from Egypt. The Christian congregation will of course want to reciprocate and invite the Jewish congregation to its services. It would be very natural on these occasions for the rabbi and minister to take public notice of the presence of their guests and the guests' clergyman. The order of worship might be explained and liturgical points of contact between synagogue and church worship emphasized.

2. Such an exchange of visits may lead the rabbi and the minister to exchange pulpits from time to time. This would give the two congregations further opportunities to notice the parallelism of their religious concerns. In addition, either congregation or both may invite the other's clergyman to give one or more lectures or Bible studies for the congregation. This would provide the opportunity to open up informal discussion of beliefs and practices that are not understood in one community or the other.

3. The congregations may discover that they have committees with identical or overlapping functions and the committees may wish to compare notes and to plan certain projects together.

The Christian congregation may have an ecumenical relations committee that serves as liaison with a council of churches and arranges special events in cooperation with other Christian congregations. Such a committee might explore ways in which the Jewish congregation might be willing and able to participate in ecumenical programs.

If the Jewish and Christian congregations have social action committees, they may find it useful and encouraging to work together, as well as with other church groups, in doing their customary work of gathering information, heightening public awareness, monitoring public agencies, securing the correction of defective public services, or providing for the better education of the public on local political issues. The Christian social action committee can make a special point of monitoring the community for any possible occurrence of antisemitic activity. The corresponding committee in the synagogue will be able to keep it informed. Up until now it has fallen to the synagogues to react to local antisemitic provocations, or perhaps to decide that it was not wise or even safe to react. How much better it will be when representatives of the Christian community—in many cases the larger and stronger community—will associate themselves with the Jewish community in making the protest, or will make the protest and call for redress in their own name as Christians!

If the Christian education committee of a congregation has a mind to examine its church school curriculum in order to see how Jews and Judaism are interpreted in it, it might like to draw the synagogue committee on Jewish education into the process. The synagogue committee will be able to supply sensitivity and correctives with reference to misunderstandings or obscurities regarding Jewish beliefs and practices, as well as literature and films that can be used in an effort to present a positive image of Jews. In fact, regardless of how good the church school's instructional materials are, it would be useful to have a rabbi address the church school teachers at least once a year and answer questions about Judaism.

There are also things that concerned clergy and laity can do in the local congregation apart from joint action with a synagogue and its committees and whether or not the denomination has provided stimulus.

4. Long before any contact is made with a synagogue committee, a concerned Christian pastor or lay person may want to study the materials used in the Sunday School and youth groups of his congregation in order to discover how they present Jews and Judaism. A reading of Olson's *Faith and Prejudice* will prepare him for this exercise; it provides numerous examples from Christian curricula of fair and unfair treatment of Jews and of no treatment at all where Christians missed opportunities to put Judaism in a good light. If he finds his own congregation's materials defective, he will probably want to interest the congregation's Christian education committee and church school teachers in setting higher standards, finding better materials, and providing special instruction for local teachers in the positive aspects of Judaism.

5. One example of putting Judaism in a positive light in the Christian fellowship is steadily to take account of the Jewish sacred calendar while proceeding through the Christian year. The Jewish festivals and fast days, like those in the Christian calendar, either commemorate great events in sacred history that are important to Christians too or deal with central themes of Jewish and Christian worship, such as repentance, confession, and forgiveness, as *Yom Kippur* does. The Christian children will usually know from their school experience that there are Jewish holidays, but not what they mean. If each of these holidays were to be given some recognition and explanation, it would become part of the Christian consciousness that Jews care about many of the same events (the exodus from Egypt) and many of the same experiences (repentance and forgiveness) that Christians do. Jews have been identified for Christians for so long in negative terms only—"they don't believe in Jesus, they

don't celebrate Christmas, or Easter." We shall have a warmer world if Jews will be identified as believing in the same God, sharing much of the same Bible, going through the same repentance, looking forward to the kingdom of God.

The newest day in the Jewish calendar, *Yom ha-Sho'ah*, the day of commemoration of the victims of the holocaust, is a grave summons to Christians to be healed of antisemitism, and is probably the most important day with which a Christian congregation can begin to become aware of the Jewish year. A local rabbi will gladly assist a Christian congregation in determining the date of *Yom ha-Sho'ah* and in discovering liturgical materials, like the *Kaddish*, appropriate to its observance.

6. Just as a Christian congregation can begin to track the Jewish calendar and observe *Yom ha-Sho' ah* without waiting for its denomination to make the suggestion, so it can also begin on its own to pray for its neighbors the Jews. At least as often as Christians pray for the whole church of Christ, that all may please God and that all may be one, so often they ought to pray for the whole biblical people of God, that Christians and Jews may love and honor one another as people of one God. It is noticeable that many Christian liturgies, echoing as they do the psalms, already frequently pray for the peace of Israel and of Jerusalem. Christians should be aware that this usage is one of the fruits of the older kind of Christian-Jewish relationship that we hope to see replaced. When this kind of liturgy was adopted, the true Israel, "the Israel of God" (Gal. 6:16), was understood to be the Christian church and the true Jerusalem, "the Jerusalem above" (Gal. 4:26). Therefore the Jews were not being prayed for at all. Prayers that will really help Christians affirm the existence of contemporary Jews as people of God will have to be written in different language.

7. It is fairly common for congregations to have libraries in which church school teachers, and members generally, can find books and films with which to improve their understanding of

their religious heritage. It is time now for such Christian libraries (and libraries that have not yet been established) to make room for literature that opens up the history and heritage of Judaism and the ongoing discussion of Christian-Jewish relations.

8. The question was raised above as to what effect an individual can have on a denomination that moves too slowly for his conscience. A concerned minister or layman who can accomplish some movement in fellowship and dialogue between his congregation and the synagogue or temple in his neighborhood acquires the experience and leverage with which to carry his concern to his regional church jurisdiction and to win further support there. If he can get his regional denominational organization to take up his concern, or even if he can win other local congregations or some of their members to share his commitment, he is on his way to making an impact on his denomination.

Any such concerned Christians should also become acquainted with Jewish and other organizations that will prove useful in the pursuit of their concern. Both the Anti-Defamation League of B'nai B'rith and the American Jewish Committee are national Jewish service organizations with regional offices and with departments of interreligious cooperation that will gladly provide Christians with understanding, cooperation, and resources. In this same connection, Christians should be aware of local Jewish community councils and local boards of rabbis (in larger cities) and of regional offices of the National Conference of Christians and Jews, all of which can be counted on to be interested.

In short, we have been dealing with a new phase of ecumenism, an ecumenism that embraces all Christians and all Jews as members of one family. Everything that Christians have learned or begun to learn from Christian ecumenism can be put to work now to bring about the reconciliation of Christians and Jews. Of course, "we need to ask . . . whether they [Jews] are willing to let us become again part of their family, a peculiar part to be sure, but, even so, relatives who believe themselves to be a peculiar kind of Jew."* Perhaps some among the Jews will not. We Christians have, unfortunately, given them good reason to be wary of Christians. But so much the more would Christians want now to be reconciled with their brothers. We are all children of the same Father.

*Krister Stendahl, "Judaism and Christianity II—After a Colloquium and a War," *Harvard Divinity Bulletin* (New Series), 1:1 (Autumn, 1967): 5, as quoted by A. Roy Eckardt, *Your People, My People* (New York: Quadrangle, 1974), p. 181.

SUGGESTIONS FOR FURTHER READING

Adler, Morris. *The World of the Talmud*. New York: Schocken Books, 1963.

Baeck, Leo. *The Essence of Judaism*. New York: Schocken Books, 1965, paperback.

———. *Judaism and Christianity*. New York: Harper & Row, 1966, Torchbook paperback.

———. *The Pharisees and Other Essays*. New York: Schocken Books, 1966, paperback.

Bokser, Ben Zion. *Judaism and the Christian Predicament*. New York: Knopf, 1967.

Cohen, Iva. *Israel: A Bibliography*. New York: Anti-Defamation League of B'nai B'rith, 1970, paperback.

Cohn, Haim. *The Trial and Death of Jesus*. New York: Harper & Row, 1971.

Conzelmann, Hans. *History of Primitive Christianity*. New York: Abingdon Press, 1973, paperback.

Danby, Herbert, ed. *The Mishnah*. London: Oxford University Press, 1933.

Eckardt, A. Roy. *Elder and Younger Brothers.* New York: Scribner, 1967, also available as Schocken paperback.

Fackenheim, Emil L. *God's Presence in History.* New York: New York University Press, 1970.

————. *Quest for Past and Future.* Bloomington: Indiana University Press, 1968.

Flannery, Edward H. *The Anguish of the Jews.* New York: Macmillan, 1965, paperback.

Flender, Harold. *Rescue in Denmark.* New York: Simon & Schuster, 1963.

Frank, Anne. *Diary of a Young Girl.* Garden City: Doubleday, 1952.

Glatzer, Nahum N. *Franz Rosenzweig, His Life and Thought.* Rev. ed. New York: Schocken Books, 1961, paperback.

————. *The Judaic Tradition.* Rev. ed. Boston: Beacon Press, 1969, paperback.

Glock, Charles Y., and Stark, Rodney. *Christian Beliefs and Anti-Semitism.* New York: Harper & Row, 1966, Torchbook paperback.

Hauer, Christian E. *Crisis and Conscience in the Middle East.* Chicago: Quadrangle Books, 1970, paperback.

Herberg, Will. *Judaism and Modern Man.* New York: Harper Torchbook paperback, 1965.

Hertzberg, Arthur, ed. *The Zionist Idea.* New York: Atheneum, 1969, also available as Harper Torchbook paperback.

Heschel, Abraham J. *Israel: An Echo of Eternity.* New York: Farrar, Straus, & Giroux, 1969, paperback.

Isaac, Jules. *Has Anti-Semitism Roots in Christianity?* New York: National Conference of Christians and Jews, 1961, paperback.

————. *The Teaching of Contempt: Christian Roots of Anti-Semitism.* New York: Holt, Rinehart & Winston, 1964.

Levin, Nora. *The Holocaust.* New York: Thomas Y. Crowell, 1968.

Long, J. Bruce, ed. *Judaism and the Christian Seminary Curriculum*. Chicago: Loyola University Press, 1965.

Margolis, Max L., and Marx, Alexander. *A History of the Jewish People*. Philadelphia: Jewish Publication Society, 1927, also available as Harper Torchbook paperback.

Montefiore, C. G., and Loewe, H., eds. *A Rabbinic Anthology*. New York: Schocken Books, 1974.

Neusner, Jacob. *Invitation to the Talmud*. New York: Harper & Row, 1973.

Olson, Bernhard E. *Faith and Prejudice*. New Haven: Yale University Press, 1963.

Opsahl, P., and Tanenbaum, M. *Speaking of God Today*. Philadelphia: Fortress Press, 1974.

Parkes, James. *The Conflict of the Church and the Synagogue*. New York: Meridian Books, 1961, paperback.

————. *A History of the Jewish People*. Rev. ed. Baltimore: Penguin Books, 1964, paperback.

Roth, Cecil. *A History of the Jews*. Rev. ed. New York: Schocken Books, 1970, paperback.

Rubinstein, Richard L. *After Auschwitz*. New York: Bobbs-Merrill, 1966.

Sandmel, Samuel. *We Jews and Jesus*. New York: Oxford University Press, 1965.

Schechter, Solomon. *Aspects of Rabbinic Theology*. New York: Schocken Books, 1961, paperback.

Schwarz-Bart, Andre. *The Last of the Just*. New York: Atheneum, 1960, also available as Bantam paperback.

Schweitzer, Frederick M. *A History of the Jews*. New York: Macmillan, 1971, paperback.

Sloyan, Gerard. *Jesus on Trial*. Philadelphia: Fortress Press, 1973, paperback.

Stark, Rodney; Foster, Bruce D.; Glock, Charles Y.; and Quinley, Harold E. *Wayward Shepherds*. New York: Harper & Row, 1971.

Steinberg, Milton. *Basic Judaism*. New York: Harcourt, Brace, & World, 1947, paperback.

Strack, Hermann L. *Introduction to the Talmud and Midrash*. New York: Harper & Row, 1965, Torchbook paperback.

Wiesel, Elie. *Night*. New York: Hill and Wang, 1960.

INDEXES

GENERAL INDEX

INDEX OF BIBLICAL REFERENCES

149

5995

BM
535
.K48   Kirsch, Paul J.

AUTHOR

WE CHRISTIANS AND JEWS

TITLE

5995